Constructing Equity

We don't need "affordable" healthcare. We need *universal* healthcare. We don't need "access" to education. We need tuition-free college and vocational training. Let's erase the weasel words and get right to the point. The only way any of us can live in a safe, healthy society is if we all do.

Freedom and equity aren't free. Neither is a stable society. We must reduce the extraordinary amount we spend on the military and demand that the ultra-wealthy and corporations pay their fair share toward the public good.

The alternative is to live in a country filled with poverty, homelessness, division, and unrest.

Every worker needs a living wage. But more than that, we need a thriving wage, and Universal Basic Income is a practical starting point.

We also need universal taxpayer-funded childcare and pre-k education, fare-free public transportation, automatic voter registration, elimination of the Electoral College, ranked choice voting, plus nationwide vote-by-mail as well as in-person voting.

We must provide training and new job opportunities for workers who will be displaced from fossil fuel industries as we confront an ever-worsening climate crisis because leaving them to fend for themselves only guarantees failure.

We pay for our choices, one way or another. Let's use our resources wisely.

Praise for Johnny Townsend

In *Zombies for Jesus*, "Townsend isn't writing satire, but deeply emotional and revealing portraits of people who are, with a few exceptions, quite lovable."

Kel Munger, *Sacramento News and Review*

In *Sex among the Saints,* "Townsend writes with a deadpan wit and a supple, realistic prose that's full of psychological empathy….he takes his protagonists' moral struggles seriously and invests them with real emotional resonance."

Kirkus Reviews

Let the Faggots Burn: The UpStairs Lounge Fire is "a gripping account of all the horrors that transpired that night, as well as a respectful remembrance of the victims."

Terry Firma, Patheos

"Johnny Townsend's 'Partying with St. Roch' [in the anthology *Latter-Gay Saints*] tells a beautiful, haunting tale."

Kent Brintnall, Out in Print: Queer Book Reviews

Selling the City of Enoch is "sharply intelligent...pleasingly complex...The stories are full of...doubters, but there's no vindictiveness in these pages; the characters continuously poke holes in Mormonism's more extravagant absurdities, but they take very little pleasure in doing so....Many of Townsend's stories...have a provocative edge to them, but this [book] displays a great deal of insight as well...a playful, biting and surprisingly warm collection."

Kirkus Reviews

Gayrabian Nights is "an allegorical tour de force...a hard-core emotional punch."

Gay. Guy. Reading and Friends

The Washing of Brains has "A lovely writing style, and each story [is] full of unique, engaging characters....immensely entertaining."

Rainbow Awards

In *Dead Mankind Walking*, "Townsend writes in an energetic prose that balances crankiness and humor....A rambunctious volume of short, well-crafted essays..."

Kirkus Reviews

Johnny Townsend

Constructing

Equity

Johnny Townsend

Printed on acid-free paper.

2023

First Edition

Cover design by Ruth Miller –
www.RuthAndJohn.com.creatives

Collected essays from

What Would Anne Frank Do?

This Is All Just Too Hard

and

Blessed Are the Firefighters

Most of the essays on race and bias from those collections have been gathered into a separate volume titled

Racism by Proxy

Contents

Introduction:
What Would Anne Frank Do?

Section One: Climate
Where Will I Go to Escape Climate Disaster Next Time?
Let's Stop Digging Our Own Graves
The LDS Church Should Create Solar and Wind Farms
We Can't *Eliminate* Our Impact on Climate, but We *Can* Lessen It
I Hope They Call Me on a Thermal Mission

Section Two: Healthcare
Why Do Democrats Deny Reality?
Give a Man a Check...
Do We Really *Need* It or Do We Just *Want* It?
The Religious Right and Right-Wing Death Panels

Section Three: LGBTQ
Love at Home with Chosen Family
Rationing Our Rights
European Programming That Broadens the LGBTQ World
Not Your Grandma's Quilt

Section Four: Race and Bias
Living in a Nun-with-a-Ruler State
Preaching to the Goddamn Choir

Section Five: Economic and Social Justice
Taxes Pay for the Nation's Physical, Not Spiritual, Needs
With Compassion Like This, Who Needs Cruelty?
Loaded Questions, Logical Fallacies, and the Presumptive
    Close Keep Us from Claiming Our Rights
Nag a Ram: Anagrams for Human Rights
Discount Human Rights
It's Risky to Nominate a Democratic Socialist: It's Also Risky
    Not To
Democratic Voters Have a New Level of Expectation
Progressives Must Accept It's OK to be Hated
Lotteries Are Essential…but They Shouldn't Be
Please Contact Me When You Have a Platform Worth
    Supporting
Zero Is Not an Increment
Zip Ties and Apron Strings

Section Six: Cultural Divide
America, We Need to Talk
The Radical Right Is America's Ammonium Nitrate
From "We'll Hide You" to "We'll Turn You In": Sowing
    Hatred and Division in the "United" States
Vote Shaming Doesn't Work, but if Reasoning Doesn't Either,
    What's Left?
I *Want* to Give You Money, But You Must Promise to Fight
    for Me
It's OK to Change Our Minds
Everything to Fear Including Fear Itself
The Cult of Trump Is the New Westboro Baptist Church
Punishing Sedition *Won't* Only Divide Us Further
We Can't Let Sunk Costs Sink Us
Want to Heal and Unify America? Then Enact Bold Change
Mormon Communists with Temple Recommends

Do Lose Friends over Politics
Joan Crawford as American History
The God Lottery
Just for the Outer Darkness of It
Who Said It Best—Republicans or Democrats?
Republicans Need to Take Responsibility for Their
      Actions…and So Do Democrats
The Democratic Party Can't Be Changed from Within
Do Extremists Just Want to Kill People They Don't Like?
Politics as Religious Conviction
Back Yard Politics is Destroying America
Does Anybody Here Know How to Fly a Plane?
What if the Current Administration is only the Warm-up Act?

Section Seven: COVID
COVID-19 Isn't My First Pandemic
Borrowed Emergency
Washing Our Hands After Using the Bathroom Isn't a Sin
Triage for an Injured America
Taking Pictures of the Tsunami
My HIV Infection Taught Me to Treat Everyone as if They're
      Contagious
Which Scrooge Are You?
COVID Blankets for Poor People
Securing the Well-Being of Citizens Is Not Tyranny
Consistent Messaging in an Emergency

Conclusion:
Keeping the Pantry Full: Freedom and Justice Demand
      Constant Vigilance

Books by Johnny Townsend
What Readers Have Said

Introduction

What Would Anne Frank Do?

When faced with a moral decision, Christians often ask themselves, "What would Jesus do?" Atheists sometimes pose the same question by quoting Christ's actual words when they feel the secular answer is more "Christian" than the mainstream religious response. The problem is that some people think Jesus would rip children away from their parents and imprison them. Others think Jesus would make sure everyone was fed, with no effort to shame the hungry in the process. Some feel that Jesus would bomb civilians. Others don't believe Jesus would be the strongest supporter of waterboarding. It's clear there are far too many answers to this question for it to be useful as a tool in guiding our behavior.

So I decided to ask myself a different one.

As a Mormon, I considered, "What would Joseph Smith do?" But even the most basic awareness of the history behind the mythology steered me away from that litmus test pretty quickly. I *didn't* want to have sex with the family babysitter in the barn.

I next considered, "What would Gandhi do?" but that possibility was ruined as well when a former bank manager told me, "We should all be like Gandhi and help people get loans."

Perhaps then it's impossible to pose the question using any historical or religious figure. But I still felt the need for a moral template and decided to give "What would Anne Frank do?" a try.

Well, Anne Frank would record everything she witnessed, wouldn't she? She'd think, she'd revise to improve the accuracy and readability of her account, she'd make the best of a bad situation and try to see the good in people.

Still, Anne Frank could be a bit of a brat, to judge by her own writings.

Martin Luther King, Jr. had lots of extramarital sex.

Laura Ingalls Wilder was biased against Native Americans.

I began wondering if perhaps we should become "cafeteria" admirers and simply pick and choose which behaviors we wanted to emulate in others. But what kind of evaluation technique could I use to help me answer that?

"What would Jesus pick and choose?"

Dagnabbit!

We've been told it isn't good to meet our heroes, that the reality always falls short of the ideal. But there's no reason we can't appreciate the good in people and follow their positive examples without condoning their sins and failures. We can ask, "What would my mother do in this situation? What would Maria's grandfather do, Levi's high school English teacher, my neighbor Cathy's ex?" and take the best examples from everyone we know when making our own decisions on difficult matters.

One evening many years ago, while walking through the French Quarter, a friend and I heard the sound of scuffling from the block ahead, and a young woman's voice calling out desperately. "Help us! Help!"

My walking companion turned the corner and headed away from the mugging. And I followed, leaving the young couple to their fate.

Far too often, we follow the *worst* aspects of other people's behavior.

Still, if I wasn't brave enough to offer assistance on my own, why didn't I at least run into a bar and call the police?

If we find ourselves more flawed than Maya Angelou, or Rabbi Akiva, or Sarah Winnemucca, we need a Plan B.

Before the pandemic, my husband Gary went door to door once a month talking to people about socialism. My friend Robert volunteered to teach English to immigrant adults. My friend Donna volunteered at a public garden. Those are all great things, but I know myself well enough to understand I simply won't do them, even if things ever "return to normal." Yet there's no value beating myself up over it. I did manage to volunteer through Jewish Family Services to play pool regularly with an elderly shut-in. I volunteered as a proofreader for a progressive Mormon magazine and a socialist newspaper. I volunteered to help prepare meals for people with HIV. I volunteered a year and a half of my time researching the Upstairs Lounge fire. I volunteered as a slush pile reader for a science fiction magazine.

And I volunteer now by writing op-eds, taking part in a community effort to find solutions to our country's most pressing problems.

We can ask what our heroes, our mentors, our friends and family, would do in any given situation, but even if *they* would make an especially good decision regarding the question at hand, it's still not necessarily what *we* should do. Or even *can* do. I'm *not* going to call prospective voters on the phone even to support causes or candidates I believe in deeply. It's not that calling folks wouldn't be the right thing, it's simply that I won't do it, so I have to find something good I *will* do.

I get so tired of seeing successful CEOs or other people in prominent positions dismiss the needs of others with, "If I can do it, so can they." No, not everyone can be a CEO. And how, exactly, would society even function in this lift-yourself-up-by-your-bootstraps scenario? All CEOs and no workers? All management and no inventors or delivery drivers or physicians or plumbers?

We can't all perform the exact same high-paying—or low-paying—job. And we can't all make the exact same decisions when faced with a moral dilemma. What we can do, though, is choose a morally appropriate response out of the several possibilities before us.

I do a decent job of listening when someone wants to tell me what they're going through. I may not have anything useful to say in response, but sometimes the help is in not saying anything at all. I can't donate $10,000 to a good cause, but I can donate $15. I may never be the world's best author, but I can say a few things in a way that's meaningful to at least some people. I can keep my mind open to other opportunities that utilize my strengths. I can choose which weaknesses to work on and when.

There's no reason we can't consider what Theodora would do in our place, what the Buddha would do, what the Gaon of Vilna would do.

These are all fair questions and could very well provide useful guidance. Reflecting on the best course of action is almost always a good idea. Ultimately, though, the only question any of us can realistically ask ourselves is this: "What will *I* look back on—the last day of my life, with my life flashing before my eyes—and wish *I* had done?"

Section One: Climate

Where Will I Go to Escape Climate Disaster Next Time?

Fifteen years ago, I grabbed my passport, birth certificate, resumé, and my checkbook. I evacuated my apartment in New Orleans with one suitcase and headed north two days before Hurricane Katrina hit. I never saw that apartment again.

If being displaced just the one time because of the worsening climate crisis was all I had to face, this might have been no more than a blip on the timeline of my life.

The loss of most of my belongings, while difficult, didn't compare to the loss of my job. I'd been with the New Orleans Public Library for four years when the hurricane struck. I figured that with a civil service job, I was relatively secure. But when your city is devastated…

So I relocated to Seattle and started over. That first winter, we endured a freak rainstorm. Living in a basement apartment on Capitol Hill, I was shocked to find water gushing through the walls, pouring down through the light fixtures. A woman in a nearby neighborhood drowned in her basement, the rising water forcing the door shut so she couldn't escape.

The last few years, though, we've faced Unhealthy and Very Unhealthy and Hazardous air quality from an increasing number of wildfires, smoke so thick I might think I was witnessing a foggy French Quarter morning. Except that I'm inhaling toxic air that stings my eyes and leaves me feeling constant heartburn, even when I'm wearing my COVID mask.

I wonder how much longer I'll be able to enjoy the refuge Seattle afforded me after I lost my hometown. Will I need to relocate again in another year? In two years?

Where will I go?

And how long will I be able to stay there?

How many thousands, or tens of thousands, or millions of other people—Americans *and* refugees from climate disaster in other countries—will be competing for housing and jobs in that next city or country I flee to?

Transitioning away from fossil fuels is difficult and expensive. Carbon capture is, too. So is finding new jobs for folks who must stop earning livelihoods from oil and gas. Transforming our consumer culture to something more sustainable will cause a sense of withdrawal far more severe than anything the pandemic has inflicted on us.

But pretending a hurricane isn't coming won't physically stop the hurricane. Ignoring warnings about the firestorm heading over the ridge doesn't actually put out the flames.

Governor Inslee ran for president as the climate candidate but couldn't muster enough votes to stay in the race through the first primary.

Neither Senators Murray nor Cantwell support a ban on fracking. Both accept campaign donations from fossil fuel corporations.

Some of our U.S. representatives and state legislators, fortunately, do refuse such campaign donations, but many more do not.

We can invest in Amazon and Boeing and Costco, but we can't seem to invest adequately in wave and thermal energy. We aren't able to retrofit our buildings with solar panels and cisterns. We're unable even to insist that these minimal improvements be required of new construction.

Sooner or later, I'll be forced to relocate. And so will a good many others in the Pacific Northwest.

But where will we go? The West Coast is burning. Siberia is burning. The Amazon is burning. Australia is burning.

The hurricane season seems to grow longer every year and, with steering currents weakening, even Category 1 storms are causing widespread destruction.

I had to travel 2600 miles to relocate the last time. How far will I need to go to find safety the next?

And what happens when there are so many of us that other countries are forced to put U.S. refugees in detention camps at their border?

It's hard to wake up and smell the Starbucks when we smell ash and soot instead.

Let's do something about it while we still can.

Let's Stop Digging Our Own Graves

A Canadian friend of mine complained that indigenous First Nations people kept refusing the jobs and industry offered them, insisting on government "handouts" instead. They should just "get over" their past abuse, he said, assimilate, and get on with life. My follow-up question was, "What kind of jobs and industry are we talking about?" Most of the industry I see on indigenous lands supports fracking and tar sands operations. Accepting such a job, no matter the salary, is like getting paid to dig your own grave.

We all know about the billions of gallons of water permanently contaminated by fracking. In a climate increasingly plagued by drought, that's no small matter. Most of the toxic chemicals are supposedly injected deep below ground to avoid polluting our drinking water, but the act of injecting water itself is directly responsible for the marked increase in earthquakes as large as 5.8 in every region where fracking takes place. And much of this "safe" drinking water is easily ignitable as it issues from residential taps.

Toxic water and damaging earthquakes aside, carbon-based fuels are the driving force behind the climate crisis. Driving faster is like thinking the solution to creating safer roadways is to speed when you see the stoplight turn yellow. Fracking also significantly increases emissions of methane, an even more potent greenhouse gas than carbon dioxide.

During World War II, Japanese soldiers often forced Filipino and American prisoners to dig their own graves. In Jim Crow times, white mobs sometimes committed this same atrocity against their black neighbors. Nazis not only forced many Jewish victims to dig their own graves, but they also forced black Allied POWs—and gays and Roma—to do so as well. Today, ISIS forces some of its victims to dig their own graves, too. It's a popular war crime.

Why would anyone agree to dig their own grave? They *know* what's going to happen when they finish. Why would they agree both to the hard work and the extreme humiliation? Why would they *help* their oppressors murder them?

People do it to buy time. Not time to be rescued. They know that won't happen. And not quality time. They get only a few awful, miserable minutes. But they are minutes of life.

So people of almost every culture, of every socioeconomic level, in conflict after conflict, agree to dig their own graves.

But some indigenous First Nations people refuse to take part in drilling. They and other activists pile barricades on railroad tracks to stop coal trains. Native Americans and other environmentalists are blocking pipeline construction in the Dakotas. Members of the

Puyallup tribe are fighting a liquified natural gas facility in Washington state. Navajo and other concerned Utahns are fighting to prevent mining and drilling on public lands. Still other Utahns are fighting Salt Lake's inland port for aiding the transportation of fossil fuels.

These folks often suffer poverty as a result. They are routinely imprisoned for protesting.

But they don't dig their own graves.

In her Emmy acceptance speech, actress Alex Borstein spoke of her grandmother being led to a pit where she would be shot and dumped along with other Jews during the Holocaust. The woman turned to her guard and asked, "What happens if I step out of line?"

The guard assured her that although he wouldn't have the heart to shoot her, someone else would.

Borstein's grandmother stepped out of line. She survived while everyone else in the group was murdered. "So step out of line, ladies," the actress told the crowd. "Step out of line."

We don't have to accept fracking and oil wells and pipelines. We don't have to dig our own graves, even if we're being paid well to do the job. And we certainly don't have to accept being shamed for choosing life over death.

Corporations driving the climate crisis have forced us all into a global catastrophe. We're scared. We're hungry. Our kids need shelter.

But they don't need the shelter provided by a tombstone or a vault. If it's an atrocity to make us dig our own graves, it's unconscionable to force us to dig those of our children.

We must refuse all new fossil fuel extraction, storage, and transport. We must step out of line if we want a fighting chance at life.

The LDS Church Should Create Solar and Wind Farms

If there's one thing the LDS Church is good at, it's acquiring real estate. Critics find this near obsession less than Christlike, but Church leaders can transform what's currently an unflattering perception into both a financial *and* PR win. The Church can convert some of its agricultural farms and cattle ranches to solar and wind farms to lessen the impact of the climate crisis. By doing so, the Church will also create more outdoor jobs, a necessity for the foreseeable future as we adapt to the new reality of social distancing in the midst of a global pandemic.

Because the LDS Church is tight-lipped about its assets, it's difficult to know exactly how many farms and ranches it owns and operates. Different sources list 290,000 acres in one part of Florida, another 380,000 acres in another part. One source lists 200,000 acres along the Utah/Wyoming border, a tract of 288,000 acres in Nebraska, and various other farms in Canada, Argentina, Brazil, and Zimbabwe. It might be easier for Church leaders to offer transparency, an act that in itself would produce good PR, if they also revealed the contributions they're making toward generating renewable energy.

The Church could hold on to its ranches and agricultural farms suffering under changing climate conditions. Or they could sell them. But they could also convert some of them to solar and wind farms. Many farmers around the world have started combining traditional crops with solar panels, sometimes even using the panels as shade for those crops vulnerable to increasing temperatures. And there's a growing variety in types of wind turbines. The Church can continue to grow crops and raise livestock where appropriate, but it can also generate and sell power to local communities.

The Church gets money. Or it can donate energy to local communities and count that as a charitable gift.

The Church reduces the community's carbon output.

The Church creates more outdoor employment.

The Church gets positive news coverage.

The Evangelical Church in Central Germany generates all the energy its various congregations need—roughly 57 million kilowatt hours—through its own wind turbines. The oldest Presbyterian church in Cleveland, Ohio, doesn't want a turbine to mar its classic 1820 structure but does purchase its energy from a nearby wind farm. In the UK, a hundred Quaker meetinghouses have embraced renewable energy sources, as have another 900 Salvation Army buildings, over 2000 Catholic parishes, and many buildings owned by the Church of England.

The roof of a single synagogue, Temple Beth El in Stamford, Connecticut, generates over 237,000 kilowatt hours of energy a year. There are solar panel and wind turbine companies that specialize in meeting the needs of religious structures.

The LDS Church claims its multi-billion-dollar portfolios are preparation for hard times. Investing to create more outdoor jobs would help address both immediate and long-term needs in the face of the pandemic. And since even more hard times will increasingly be related to climate change, why not add investments in solar and wind power to Church portfolios? Why not add carbon capture technologies? These and other "green" enterprises are where future income lies, not fossil fuels.

The Church can also invest in geothermal power and wave energy. It can add solar panels to some of their chapels. A solitary wind turbine on every Church property could become as much of a signature as Moroni atop LDS temples. All of these actions would add to global efforts at tackling the climate crisis, making them essential *regardless* of public perception. But they'll *also* create goodwill.

Each president of the Church wants to leave a personal legacy. David O. McKay is known for bringing the 19th century Church into the 20th century. Spencer W. Kimball is known for greatly expanding the missionary program. Gordon B. Hinckley is known for his great strides in reducing societal stigma surrounding the Church.

President Nelson can be known for changing the name of the Mormon Tabernacle Choir. Or he can be known for being the tech president, for bringing the Church into the 21st century and leading the worldwide religious efforts to address our ever more desperate climate emergency, which threatens more lives and livelihoods than even the worst-case projections for the coronavirus outbreak. And that's a lot.

By their fruits ye shall know them.

Let's pray for some climate-friendly fruit.

We Can't *Eliminate* Our Impact on Climate, but We *Can* Lessen It

Some climate activists grow discouraged when they discover that wind, solar, wave, and thermal energy technologies each carry their own damaging limitations. But that's no reason to give up on renewables. The only way to completely eliminate the negative consequences of human activity on the planet…is to eliminate humans. Short of that, the best we can do is reduce the damage. A transition away from fossil fuels is an essential step forward.

Harm reduction is a term describing the effort to help those addicted to drugs without expecting to solve the problem. For instance, while it's better if a person stops shooting up altogether, if that's not feasible simply by hoping or praying—or punishing—then the next best thing is to make shooting up less destructive. We provide clean needles and a "safe" place to inject, perhaps have someone nearby ready with naloxone. It's not ideal, but if we can reduce some of the worst consequences of addiction, we have a better chance at reaching the most vulnerable and eventually finding better solutions.

Michael Moore's film *Planet of the Humans* suggests technology isn't an answer to the climate crisis. We must instead significantly decrease the global population and live in harmony with nature. Is the solution then to bioengineer a more powerful disease than COVID-19? Carbon emissions had begun rising significantly even by the year 1900, when there were fewer than two billion people on the planet. It might be difficult to rally people behind killing four or five billion of their fellow man. Even if all 7.7 billion of us here today gave up technology, we'd *still* create havoc with the environment. It would be a different type of damage, and maybe a lesser one in regard to carbon, but we'd still leave our mark, and it wouldn't be pretty.

Remember how the fields at Woodstock looked in 1969?

All other things being equal, what's better for a forest? Cutting down twenty-four trees or three hundred and sixty-two?

What's a better outcome for a nuclear war? Three destroyed cities or seven hundred?

Would you rather your hometown suffer a 5.1 magnitude earthquake or an 8.4?

A simplified example of chaos theory is the butterfly flapping its wings in China and then through a series of unpredictable cause and effect repercussions, it rains in France. The truth is we're *going* to have a negative impact on the environment and climate. We *can*, though, mitigate the damage. That mitigation will inevitably cause unexpected damage, and we'll need to find a way to lessen that. Then *that* mitigation will need tweaking as well. But we don't give up making improvements just because the next step forward isn't 100% perfect.

Perhaps we can't stop the impact of all fossil fuel extraction already in process, but we can certainly refuse to add to the problem. When our frying pan catches fire while we're cooking dinner, we don't pour a bottle of vegetable oil on it to douse the flames. We don't pour water, either. But there *are* options to limit the damage.

We must immediately stop making the worst climate choices possible—oil, coal, fracking, even nuclear with its radioactive waste and potential for sabotage.

Do we refuse to support renewable energy technology because it's developed and sold by corporations? Waiting until the U.S. and other capitalist countries convert to socialism before we begin a full-fledged transition away from fossil fuels is suicide. Yes, it may take such a conversion to repair the worst damage, but we can't wait until conditions are perfect before we take action.

We certainly can't wait a hundred years for a global one-child policy to reduce the human population to a healthier level, as essential as that may be in an overall plan.

Our best options at the moment for reducing the catastrophic impact of our presence on the planet are wind, solar, wave, and thermal energy technologies. But even if we completely convert the entire globe to these renewables in the next ten years, that will hardly be the end of human progress. Technology didn't stop with the invention of the wheel or the discovery of fire. It didn't end with pulleys or levers or the steam engine. And it won't stop when we transition away from fossil fuels.

This adaptation *cannot possibly* be perfect. Neither will the next one or the one after that.

None of that means it's okay to construct a single new pipeline or drill even one more well.

We can't eliminate greed or stupidity, either, but we'd sure better find a way to lessen their destructive impact.

Or perhaps we *will* choose a massive human death toll, after all. By default.

Harm reduction works for people and it works for climate, too. So let's develop the renewables we can and start reducing harm before we overdose on the status quo.

I Hope They Call Me on a Thermal Mission

As I watched entire planeloads of Mormon missionaries returning early, I wondered aloud to my RM husband, "How is Church culture going to handle losing this rite of passage?" Record numbers of young men have already been returning home early these past few years, more and more choosing not to serve a mission at all. Anecdotal evidence (the only evidence available given the Church's secrecy) suggests members in general have been leaving the Church "in droves."

But perhaps there's a way the Church can survive both the coronavirus and the abundance of information easily accessible via the internet.

The LDS Church has a long history of accomplishing incredible feats, from the settling of the intermountain west to photographing genealogical records across the world to sending out tens of thousands of volunteer missionaries every year. During the COVID-19 pandemic, the Mormon Church can use its organizational skills and devoted membership to help society transition away from fossil fuels by calling young men and women to serve as "renewable energy missionaries."

We've already shown we can make tremendous changes almost overnight. No more General Conference gatherings, no more weekly church meetings, no more early morning Seminary, no more temple work.

But committed members of the Church still want to serve, and Church leaders can channel that energy and dedication in other positive directions. Since the climate crisis threatens more death and destruction than even worst-case scenarios for the coronavirus, we have no choice but to transition toward renewables. And since the Church cannot send missionaries on proselyting missions anytime soon, the Church, the members, and the world can all benefit from calling members to transform Church ranches and agricultural farms into wind, solar, and even thermal energy farms.

In the long history of Mormon missionary work, we've adapted many times already. We've sent men into the world "without purse or scrip," sent men on three-year missions, sent missionaries out with no language training, sent women out as well, changed the age for missionary service, sent out married couples, sent missionaries to construct chapels, sent out "health" missionaries, sent missionaries out to do a wide variety of tasks apart from proselyting.

For the foreseeable future, we'll need more outdoor employment. The Church can acquire thousands of hours of labor from volunteers to help defray the cost of the necessary energy conversion. This type of missionary work will also teach young people job skills they'll need after the global depression we are likely to experience.

Calling members on renewable energy missions is a victory on every level.

Older folks who wish to serve, or younger folks with physical limitations, can still do so by handling supply orders or monitoring information or performing other functions that don't require heavier physical labor.

And some missionaries, of course, can still serve online missions. Perhaps even these renewable energy missionaries can spend one day a week proselyting online. Others can sharpen their persuasive skills and then petition state and federal governments to do their part in helping society transition to renewables. Proselyting missionaries are essentially lobbyists anyway. The Missionary Training Center's teaching program won't require much adaptation at all—other than a shift to more online learning. There is much work to be done by a volunteer missionary workforce, all of which benefits the Church and its members both now and in the future.

I served two years as a missionary forty years ago. It remains one of the most profound experiences of my life more than three decades after I left the Church. I belong to a Facebook group for those who served under my mission president, and I'm astounded that several of the young men and women I didn't expect to remain active more than a few months after they returned home are *still* devout members all these years later.

Missionary work can bring converts to the Church, but that's not its only function. It also helps young men and women take an active, meaningful part in a noble endeavor. They work hard, they sacrifice, and they are permanently changed by the process. If Church leaders want their young people to stay committed to the organization, they need to begin offering something genuinely useful that can counterbalance the secularization of society and the unrelenting availability of unexpurgated Church history online.

Door to door, in-person missionary work will not be feasible for quite some time and might be doomed even apart from the current pandemic. But the Church can still serve its members and the rest of the world by channeling the devotion and goodwill of its missionaries into helping society transition to renewables, an evolution we *must* make in the next few years regardless.

Mormons pride themselves on being the same in every congregation around the world. We teach the same lessons, sing the same hymns, read the same scriptures, believe the same doctrine. But Mormons also have two centuries of major adaptation. Moving from New York to Pennsylvania to Ohio to Missouri to Illinois to Utah, transitioning from monogamy to polygamy to monogamy, even transitioning from hiding the history of the First Vision to becoming more transparent.

We can do this.

Let's start calling members to serve renewable energy missions.

Section Two: Healthcare

Why Do Democrats Deny Reality?

We ask the question every day: "Why do conservatives deny reality?" We're baffled that many can't accept the reams of evidence proving climate change. We're mortified when some insist the Holocaust never happened. We watch in horror while dying patients gasp for air in the ICU, whispering, "I can't have COVID. It's a hoax."

As a progressive, I realize conservatives won't listen to me. So I have a different question. Why do *Democrats* deny reality?

"Single-payer healthcare will cost $34 trillion over the next ten years. Where will you get the money to pay for that?"

"Healthcare in the U.S. already costs $3.6 trillion a year. The projections you're quoting come from multiple studies, including one conducted by a right-wing think tank, that show we'd instead save *money by adopting a single-payer system, as well as guarantee care to every American."*

"You didn't answer my question! Where will you get the money?"

"Your real question was, 'Is a single-payer system feasible?' And I answered that."

"You wannabe socialists are all alike. You dodge the hard questions."

"Any bill submitted to Congress to create a single-payer system would likely be 600 or more pages long. Are you granting me the time in this on-air sound bite interview to provide you the facts and figures from 600 pages of material? Time before you break for commercial to quote the numbers from those twenty-two studies already available to you?"

"I repeat—how are you going to pay for a $34 trillion dollar program?"

"It's $3.4 trillion a year, not $34 trillion. Using the ten-year cost is deliberately misleading. You might as well ask how we're going to pay $340 trillion over a hundred years. You do realize, don't you, that every other industrialized nation in the world already has some form of universal healthcare? You realize that some of those countries have had their universal healthcare programs for several decades? You realize the citizens of those countries have better health outcomes on average than Americans? Longer life spans? Lower child mortality? You realize that citizens in many of those countries score much higher on surveys measuring happiness?"

"So you're not going to answer my question."

"The question has been answered—by the UK, by France, by Spain, by Germany, by Sweden, by Norway, by

two dozen other countries. The U.S. has more resources than almost any other nation in the world. If all those other countries can accomplish this, why are you so convinced we can't? It's not as if we're proposing a colony on Mars or trying to clone dinosaurs."

Such a discussion could go on indefinitely...probably for 600 pages. The bottom line, of course, is that a conservative mask denier is not substantially different from an elected official or corporate news anchor who denies the reality of successful universal healthcare programs across the globe.

When Democrats refuse to ban fracking, when they refuse to support tuition-free college and vocational training, when they refuse to provide guaranteed childcare, refuse to raise the minimum wage, refuse even to consider a Universal Basic Income, they are refusing to acknowledge reality.

If it's bad when Republicans do it, it's also bad when Democrats do it. It's bad when religious folks do it, when atheists do it, when both uneducated and educated people do it. If Democrats want to believe Republicans are worse, that conservatives deny even more reality than Democrats do, that's fine. It's probably true. But that doesn't mean the realities those on the left are denying aren't important, too.

It's not OK to deny that healthcare, education, and a livable environment are human rights.

It's not OK to deny that ensuring human rights costs money, not OK to insist that anyone pushing for justice somehow make equality cost-free.

We all have blind spots. That's natural, human. But if our blind spot covers 70% of our field of vision, that's a problem.

If it makes Democratic leaders—or voters—feel good to ridicule the stupidity of science-denying Republicans, let's do so if we must.

But our self-esteem will grow much stronger if we stop living in denial ourselves.

Give a Man a Check...

We've all heard the saying, "Give a man a fish, feed him for a day. Teach a man to fish and feed him for a lifetime." Helping someone care for their own needs rather than just offering a handout is clearly the better approach. And yet many on the right feel that *any* taxpayer-funded program that helps people take care of themselves is somehow instead hurting them. One of my former missionary colleagues describes most of this "purported" aid as "giving someone a check," insisting that the only thing it accomplishes is to make the recipient feel both entitled and dependent. Perhaps we should rephrase the left's approach in a more relatable way. "Give people a check, pay their bills for a month. Teach people job skills and let them pay their own bills for life."

If the U.S. could offer its citizens tuition-free college and vocational training, as many other nations do, no student need get "a check" at all. Students instead gain access to classrooms and teachers. They gain access to information, tutoring, labs, and fieldwork. They gain access to job and career competency so they can succeed in the workplace and provide for themselves and their families. This means a reduction in demand for taxpayer dollars directed to food assistance or subsidized housing. A reduction in demand for funds directed to jails and prisons filled with those spurred to find "alternate" methods of employment.

If the U.S. could offer its citizens genuine socialized healthcare, lowering the cost of drugs and medical supplies as an essential ingredient, as a nation we'd spend far less on healthcare than we do now. Those are funds that can be spent on consumer goods, on renewable energy research, on roads and bridges. With guaranteed healthcare (and guaranteed sick leave), fewer workers would need to come to work sick, spreading their cold or flu or COVID. There would be less absenteeism, more productivity. No one will be "giving a check" to someone to see a doctor, with the accompanying suspicion the recipient might run off to the racetrack instead. The ill person simply gets to seek medical care without having to worry about not having enough of his or her own funds left over to pay the light bill.

"But if we just let people get all the education they want and all the healthcare they need, they'll be spoiled brats. They won't appreciate how good they have it."

To be fair, that's a real possibility. But right now, the privileged children of rich parents get a good education and all the medical care they want, and no one seems to mind. There are no laws forcing all college students to pay their own way without any assistance from their parents or from scholarships or grants, forcing everyone over eighteen off their parents' insurance. Why are those on the right only worried about the gratitude of the masses? If getting an education without groveling is good enough for children of the wealthy, why do the rest of us have to clean toilets eight hours every night for the same privilege?

Why is it so, so important for peasants never to forget their place?

So they won't dare to rise out of it?

The truth is that students from low-income areas almost never receive the early education they need to succeed in college, even if they do manage to find a job that will allow them to earn the application fee. Adult children of the moneyed elite often turn out to be pretty awful human beings, but it's only the grown kids of the poor that we like to label "losers." If "giving someone a check" is so destructive to the poor, we'd have to believe that *not* helping them has proven a well-traveled path to virtue. And yet we've been judging and condemning these folks all of our lives for their moral failings.

Since *not* providing a good education hasn't worked either to improve the character of the poor *or* allow them skills to provide for themselves, maybe we've chosen a different motto altogether than the one we've enshrined. "Don't give a man a fish, starve him for a day. Refuse to teach him how to fish and starve him for a lifetime."

It's not as if folks who can't afford tuition are asking for honorary degrees.

Those on the right often demand that recipients of government assistance be working to qualify. And then make it almost impossible for the unskilled to get a job, especially when the job pays such low wages they can't even earn enough to cover childcare while they're working.

A society of educated, competent citizens with full access to healthcare is better for everyone, even if the newly educated and competent end up with a little attitude. Because let's face it, what we have now is a society filled with desperate, unhappy people lacking the education or healthcare they need, and there's still more than enough attitude to go around.

We may never be able to guarantee our citizens a good moral character. Let's leave that up to religion and other organizations. What the state *can* do, and must, is make sure we all have the education and medical care to succeed in life, and that we have at least the remote chance of being happy about it when we do.

Do We Really *Need* It or Do We Just *Want* It?

We all remember Mom or Dad asking us, "Do you really *need* that or do you just *want* it?" Our leaders don't seem to understand that when we say we need programs like Medicare for All, we aren't spoiled brats throwing a tantrum because we can't get the shiny toy Becky down the street has. Do we *want* Medicare for All? Of course we do. But that's because we *need* it.

If we ever needed proof that tying health insurance to the workplace is a bad idea, it's during a pandemic killing tens of thousands of people and hospitalizing even more. Right as more than 16 million Americans lose their jobs—and any health insurance that came along with it, the presumptive Democratic nominee for president is dismissing universal healthcare as a fundamental right. But those 16 million workers aren't the only Americans without healthcare. Their children are without it now as well. *And* the 30 million others who are *already* un- or underinsured.

My sister, a nurse in a nursing home, doesn't get health insurance from her employer. She hasn't had health insurance in years. Does she *want* medical coverage or does she *need* it?

While Medicare for All might be the most obvious need Americans have, it's certainly not the only item on our ~~Want~~ Need List.

Almost every other industrialized nation in the world offers their citizens (and even many non-citizens) tuition-free college. Here in the U.S., we tell prospective students that if they want an education bad enough, they need to take out a student loan that may sink them in debt for thirty years. If they want to be low-life bums, though, without any education or vocational skills, that's their choice, and they need to live with the consequences. The question for our political leaders is this—Do we as a nation *need* forty million uneducated adults in the workforce or do we just *want* chronic unemployment and poverty? A follow-up question might be—Do we *want* to deal with the consequences of having that uneducated workforce or have we simply created a society where we *need* to?

Do we merely want to reduce carbon emissions or do we need to?

Do we need to incarcerate a larger percentage of our population than any other nation or do we just want to?

Do we need a voting system that disenfranchises large portions of the electorate or do we just want one?

Do we need a homelessness crisis or do we just want one?

Do we need to separate the children of asylum seekers from their parents or do we just want to?

Do we want clean drinking water or do we need it?

We have made choices as a nation that answer every one of these questions and more. We've chosen to create ignorance and poverty. We've chosen to perpetuate illness and misery. We've chosen to create and maintain economic injustice, racism, and sexism. Those conditions didn't just "happen." We *made* them happen.

It's all too clear that Republican leaders don't want to address these problems, but by consistently pushing pro-corporate, anti-worker policies on us, Democratic leaders tell us time and again *they* don't want to address them, either. They understand that they need to give lip service to solutions, that they need to make token advancements, but they don't want to adopt policies that would all but eliminate them.

As voters, we don't *need* Bernie Sanders or Elizabeth Warren or Alexandria Ocasio-Cortez or any other specific person. What we do need are humane policies. DNC leaders, you need to hear this: you can give us whatever candidates you want, but if you don't give us the solutions and programs we need, *you* need to understand that there are political consequences.

You should *want* to avoid them.

The Religious Right and Right-Wing Death Panels

When the Affordable Care Act was up for a vote during President Obama's first term, the cry from right-wing opponents was that "Obamacare" would create "death panels." Bureaucrats would sit in meeting rooms deciding if Grandma got to live or not. Socialized medicine, which the ACA is not, would be even worse. Only capitalism cares about Grandma's life. It wasn't true then—as insurance execs sat in meeting rooms determining which patients would receive treatment and which would be left to die—and it's certainly not true now as right-wing "Re-open the economy!" advocates prove.

Several of my religious friends have strongly criticized temporary workplace closings to flatten the curve during the early part of the pandemic. Two of them, both physicians, characterized the situation as "destroying the economy to save old people who would have been dead in two weeks anyway." But that rationale, even if it were accurate, raises an important religious/political question: if we don't care about those last two weeks of Grandma's life now, was it OK before the pandemic, and will it be OK again afterward, for families to euthanize Grandma when it looks like she's getting close to the end? And if it *is* OK, would its acceptability be based on pain and quality of life or would it be based on economic concerns?

One can't always tell if an 81-year-old is going to die in the next few weeks. She could live another ten or fifteen years. Valerie Harper (Rhoda from *The Mary Tyler Moore Show*) was diagnosed with lung cancer in 2009. Would it have been OK to write her off then? She was still alive in 2013, when the cancer spread to her brain and she was given three months to live. Surely, at that point, it would be OK to consider the remainder of her life meaningless. "No one's giving up a haircut for you!"

But in 2016, she was still working on film projects. She did not die until the end of August 2019.

So at what point would it have been acceptable for Valerie to willingly choose physician-assisted death on her own behalf? At what point would it have been acceptable for her family to decide that for her? And if neither she nor her family had that right, why do Republicans feel entitled to claim it for themselves, magnanimously sacrificing the lives of people they don't even know? After all, they can hardly limit the sacrifice to their own parents, regardless of how much they might stand to inherit. They are making this decision for *everyone*.

If suicide is a sin, why doesn't the religious right put up a fuss when they hear an elderly person offer themselves as a sacrifice to the economy? Is someone else's suicide only acceptable when it benefits you? Why do so many of the faithful pressure the old and sick to willingly give up their God-given right to live a decent life for as long as they can?

Recently, a right-wing pundit said he was willing to eat his neighbors and feed them to his children if he had to. His superpower, he boasted, was honesty. What he didn't add was that this push to "Re-open the economy!" while unprepared means he's also willing to throw 100,000 additional grandmas into the maw of corporations just to briefly assuage their insatiable hunger.

Of course, Americans of the religious right don't want to kill the old and sick themselves. They just want to "let" them die. They want "nature" to "take its course" so life can go on…for the people who matter.

If this was just an either/or proposition, perhaps they might even be right. But it isn't. We could choose to send monthly checks to every worker until the pandemic was under control. Such a program would cost less than the trillions given to corporations. And even if we insisted on giving money primarily to these corporations, we could still choose to make the bailouts contingent on corporations paying their employees. There are a variety of other options to explore as well.

But for the religious right, sending someone a check just for sitting at home not infecting anyone is a sin far worse than senilicide, worse than euthanizing the disabled, worse than terminally ill patients requesting medication to allow them the luxury of dying painlessly on a timeline of their choosing.

No, the only moral course of action is to let Grandma, and Grandpa, and Aunt Sally, and Cousin Joe suffer for three weeks on a ventilator before dying. If healthcare professionals also get sick and die, or bring it home to their family causing some of their loved ones to die, well, they all knew what they were getting into when they applied to nursing programs and medical schools. And if hospital custodians get sick and die, too, no one forced them to get a job at a medical facility. Besides, it's not a sin to let poor people die naturally, is it? That's just "life."

If "the economy" is more important than the lives of anyone who "might" die in the next few months or years, why not just kill everyone outright who reaches the age of 65 or 70? No one needs to battle over Social Security anymore. Think of the money we could save by not wasting it on these mostly unproductive people. And that's just their pensions. There are tens of billions more to save every year by no longer wasting medical treatment on people who are doomed to die relatively soon no matter how much we spend on them.

We might as well round up and euthanize all the homeless people, too. Think of the millions we could save, how lovely our cities could be without them. Pretending that all human life deserves equal respect is just a big waste of money. Even worse, it's inconvenient.

Americans are happy with politicians who dedicate a trillion dollars a year to the military because that outrageous expense will "save lives." So why does money matter *now* to save our most vulnerable? Do we only stand up for others when it's easy?

We don't have to sacrifice the economy to save the most vulnerable in our community. We don't have to sacrifice the most vulnerable in our community to save the economy.

We might, however, need to sacrifice corporate welfare.

That's a death panel we should all want to be on.

Section Three: LGBTQ

Love at Home with Chosen Family

As we try to recover from the last several acrimonious years, we need to be judicious in where and how we spend our time and emotional energy.

As a Mormon missionary, I used to ask people, "Don't you want to be with your family for eternity?" Mormons, obviously, were the only people on the face of the Earth who held the key to this blessing.

As the years passed, though, I found it harder and harder even to send Christmas cards to my biological family. This holiday season, there are some family members I simply won't send cards to at all, even if they send me one.

I don't *like* many of the people I'm supposed to want to spend eternity with. They're not worth a Forever stamp.

When I see other ex-Mormons on Facebook ask if they should maintain contact with believing family members who ostracize and judge them, I'm mystified when people advise, "Don't throw away love and blood ties for differences of opinion."

But if it's the "opinion" of my family that I'm going to spend eternity in Outer Darkness, if it's their opinion that I'm one of the main reasons the country is falling apart, if they believe that the world would be better off if people like me didn't exist or, at the very least, didn't have any rights, I'm not sure I'm throwing much "love" away. If there are any "ties" left, they are for binding me, not sustaining me.

Of course, these conflicts don't just exist between Mormons and ex-Mormons. They exist among people of all faiths and in secular families as well. They exist when people hold fundamentally different beliefs in how they view human suffering and what to do about it.

When I told my cousin I was writing a book about the Upstairs Lounge fire, an arson which killed 32 people in a French Quarter gay bar, her response wasn't one of horror at the atrocity committed against other human beings. She said, with a tone of disgust, "They died in a *bar?*"

During a casual discussion of missionary experiences with family members, I mentioned something about my "two years in Italy." Another of my cousins, born just a few months before I left for the Missionary Training Center, interjected forcefully, "Eighteen months!"

I stopped and stared. During my mission, the First Presidency changed the length of full-time missions for men from two years to eighteen months. My twenty-two months constituted an "honorable" mission in every way. Women were called to eighteen-month missions as a rule, and no one in my family felt it necessary to diminish their service. The "proper" duration of foreign missions in the past had been three years, and no one chastised my uncle for only having served two years abroad.

The *only* reason to disrespect and dismiss my full-time volunteer work for the Church was that I had since left the fold.

It was *important* to my cousin that I understand I was inferior.

Even more distressing was the realization that my inadequate missionary performance had clearly been a topic of conversation multiple times in that household. I was and would always be "less than" in their eyes.

Still, friends told me that after years of patience and perseverance, their families had eventually come around, so I kept visiting, I kept calling, I kept emailing and sending holiday cards.

And then one day, I realized that I was always the one initiating contact. If I waited for family members to contact me, perhaps that would reveal whether or not they even wanted me to keep in touch.

So I waited. And waited and waited.

A couple of years later, a family member did send a card, mentioning an injury she'd sustained over a year earlier in a car accident. I could see she felt I didn't care because I hadn't called or written at the time of the accident. It didn't occur to her that I hadn't called because no one in her family had let me know anything had happened.

In her mind, in the minds of her family, I would always be the bad guy, always the insensitive one, always the one responsible for any hurt or misunderstanding.

I'm not "Friends" with most of my family, so their posts don't show up on my Facebook feed. And I try to avoid FB as much as possible in any event because I think it introduces more harm than good to the world. But once in a while, I plug in a relative's name and check their latest posts.

Dipping my toe in the water to test the temperature.

I see rants against Black people or an adamant disbelief in climate change or "funny" jokes insulting people who believe in universal healthcare.

It doesn't matter to me that they've been deceived, either by their religious leaders or their chosen news network. I was raised in the same religion, with the same conservative political beliefs. But I was able to read and listen and pay attention and think and change my mind when I gained more information. And commit to additional learning and reassessment as I continue on.

They've chosen not to do that.

I miss my family. I miss being in harmony with them, having the same beliefs and goals. But that time has come and gone. I do not have enough years left to worry about it.

I will never have my baby teeth again. My hair will never again have natural pigment.

Even if family members who'd said the most hateful things were to "see the light" and apologize, our relationships have already been altered beyond repair. I'd wish them well in their new enlightened state, but they simply don't feel like family any longer.

"You can't go home again."

When I see movies set in today's Italy, I'm struck by the changes that have taken place in the four decades since I left. While watching one film, I listened as a character said something that made me realize he didn't understand what life in his own country was like the year he was born.

I know more about Italy in 1980 than a forty-year-old man who's lived there his entire life.

I wasted too many years trying to reconcile my affectional orientation with my religion. I wasted too many decades trying to maintain a relationship with my biological family.

Thankfully, I've also invested in chosen family over the past thirty years.

As a Mormon missionary, I was confronted by the reality that I couldn't save everyone. As a gay democratic socialist, I realize I can't "connect" with everyone on "the left."

How much more might I have been able to accomplish over the years if I hadn't thrown away so much valuable time and energy on relationships doomed to petty attacks and judgments?

We don't need to placate "conservatives" in our families, in the Republican Party, or even in the Democratic Party. Republicans will not "like" us or move to the left just because we're nice to them and give up our power to show how sincere we are.

"Moderate" Democrats won't like us for being "humble" or "reasonable" or "pragmatic" by giving in to them. They'll take everything we offer and still disrespect us.

Since we don't have unlimited amounts of time, money, patience, and energy, we need to devote our efforts toward chosen family—in both our personal and political lives.

Rationing Our Rights

On Thanksgiving Day 1981, I was a Mormon missionary living in Naples, and our mission president allowed us to spend the holiday with Americans stationed at the US Navy base near Capodichino. Sister Costantino had come with her American companion and spoke no English. But she was able to point out how romanticizing our superiority led us to ignore reality.

When the radio played Neil Diamond's "America," she asked me to translate the lyrics. I'd hardly made it through three lines before she threw up her hands in irritation. "You Americans think you're the only people in the world with freedom. Even Italians have some freedoms you don't have."

Back in America, I was again captivated by the moving music as it played over the opening credits of "The Jazz Singer." The scenes showed people from every ethnicity and religion living and working together in New York City, the lyrics proudly declaring that America was a beacon of hope and light, that people from everywhere came to this great country to share in its riches, opportunities, and "liberty."

I continued to believe in our superior humanity for years. As a white, middle-class male, I did enjoy many opportunities and freedoms, so it wasn't apparent to me that others living just down the street did not. And now, when I see the "Proud Boys" burning Black Lives Matter banners during a pro-Trump rally, it's clear yet again that far too many white people see rights as a zero-sum game. They can't accept the president's loss because they see it as a loss of *their* personal rights. They believe there aren't enough rights to go around, that we need a human rights austerity program to ration our rights.

I can't imagine a greater lack of faith in America than to believe we have so few freedoms that only a privileged portion of our citizenry can be allowed to enjoy them.

Latter-day Saints and members of other conservative religions believe there is only so much marriage to go around. If we allow same-sex marriage, then some heterosexual couples won't be allowed to marry. Obviously, we must ration the right to marry.

Everyone understands there's a limited supply of love. You know, the way a mother can only love two of her children, even if she has six.

If we fund majority Black or brown public schools as fully as we fund majority white public schools, white students somehow won't have access to all the information they currently do. There's only so much knowledge available to spread around.

And can we imagine the dystopia our nation would be reduced to if we guaranteed a college education or vocational training to every adult in the country? Why, why, we'd…have a fully educated and trained work force.

Many conservatives seem to feel that liberals shouldn't have the right to vote. Black Americans shouldn't have the right to vote. Naturalized citizens from certain countries shouldn't have the right to vote. If *they're* allowed to vote, then the votes of white conservatives are automatically worth less.

But the votes of white people are not worth less. The votes of Mormons aren't worth less. The votes of Christians aren't worth less.

Everyone's votes are simply equal. And there's more than enough equality to go around.

I was called to serve as a missionary in Rome, where our message promised that Italian Catholics, Jews, Muslims, and atheists were all equally worthy to be baptized and share fully in "the gospel." We taught Romanian refugees and immigrants from Ghana and Nigeria. Everyone was to be treated the same, poor families in the slums of Napoli and middle-class families in Ciampino.

As a Mormon, as an American, I believed in equality and fairness and acceptance and inclusion. We were all one great, big eternal family.

I'm an ex-Mormon now, excommunicated because I dared to love another man. But I'm still American, and I still believe in equality and fairness and acceptance and inclusion.

Latter-day Saints continue to remain free to practice whatever doctrine they wish, are free to exclude anyone from their congregations they choose. They are free to vote for conservative political candidates. They are free to plan for the Millennium when the world will be run as a theocracy. They are free to plan for their futures in the Celestial Kingdom, where everyone will behave just as they are supposed to.

When *I* was a Mormon, I still believed that non-Mormons had rights.

The most disappointing discovery of my life was that so many other Mormons didn't feel the same. When I listen to my family and former missionary pals praise Trump and, worse, utter *not one word* against his attempt to stage a coup and overturn a lawful election, not a word against the violence being encouraged against their fellow Americans, I think back on that Thanksgiving Day almost forty years ago.

And I can't understand why so many people insist on rationing peace.

European Programming that Broadens the LGBTQ World

I stumbled upon MHz while flipping channels and was immediately captivated by an attractive man speaking Italian. Since my husband and I had lived in Italy for two years as Mormon missionaries, I set down the remote and watched. *Nero Wolfe*, an adaptation of Rex Stout's mystery novels given a new setting in Rome, was playing. I soon learned that MHz hosted a broad range of European programming, utilizing white subtitles with a thin, dark border that allows them to be fully legible no matter what background they're up against. While sexism is evident in almost every European series I've watched so far, many of the leads are strong women and quite a few shows depict LGBTQ characters matter-of-factly, without judgment, even in period pieces. There's also a series of French shorts, *Bureau of Sexist Affairs*, explicitly about modifying unacceptable sexist behavior. My husband and I now watch MHz almost every evening.

Given our background, we focused first on television series set in Italy. In addition to *Nero Wolfe*, MHz offers *Murders at Barlume*, *Inspector Manara*, *Detective Montalbano*, and *Bulletproof Heart*. *Inspector Vivaldi* showcases a father-son investigative team, the son an out gay man. Another series, *Luisa Spagnoli*, set in the early

20th century, tells the true story of a determined woman who builds the world-famous Perugina chocolate factory with the help of a gay mentor.

The star of *Imma Tataranni* looks just like a former partner of mine, from the same region in southern Italy where the show is set, if he'd ever done drag. *The Bastards of Pizzofalcone* reminds me of my time knocking on doors in Naples. *Song of Napoli* shows me the life I *wish* I'd led while there.

Transitioning northward, *Donna Leon's Brunetti*, set in Venice, is produced in German, odd initially, but no different really than watching the HBO series *Rome* with English-speaking actors. Quite a few other shows are set in Germany, Austria, and Switzerland. *The Undertaker* gives us a former detective who takes over his father's funeral parlor but can't resist investigating suspicious deaths. *Crime Scene Cleaner* shows us the daily life of an everyman hired to clean up the mess left when someone dies. It's a comedy, in case that wasn't obvious.

French programs on MHz are among the most entertaining offered. While the personality conflicts we witness time and again in the series *Murder In* sometimes feel formulaic, we do see extraordinary settings and a variety of French sub-cultures. *Detectives* is charming, set in Paris, and stars polyglot Sara Martins of BBC's *Death in Paradise* (she also speaks Portuguese). Agatha Christie's *Criminal Games*, set in northern France of the late 1950s, gives us a sexist investigator, his Marilyn Monroe-wannabe secretary, and a "scrappy" young reporter traumatized by her upbringing in an orphanage. All three are both appalling and lovable. Irrelevant factoid: Elodie Frenck, the Peruvian-Swiss-French actress who plays the secretary, is a survivor of the 2004 tsunami in southeast Asia.

A new MHz offering is *Speakerine*, set in Paris of the early '60s, with hints of *All About Eve* if it had been directed by Hitchcock. We get seven seasons of *A French Village*, taking us through the occupation of World War II. It doesn't hurt that casting choices in most of these shows are often more varied than is the case in the U.S., with a little person as a lead investigator or other main characters who might be heavier, older, or not as traditionally attractive as the casting required by many U.S. studios.

Several seasons of *Velvet*, set in Franco's fascist Spain, give us a love story to illustrate class conflict. *Daughter of the Law*, from Portugal, is quite shocking (no spoilers, but be prepared for *anything*). There's a Dutch mystery, a thriller set in Afghanistan, the fascinating *Borgen* from Denmark, and a German/Turkish version of *The Brady Bunch* called *Turkish for Beginners.* Many of the northern European shows are rather dark—take your preferred medication before attempting Sweden's *Wallander* or Finland's *Vares.*

Still, the Swedish *Miss Friman's War*, set in the early 20th century, tells a slightly less harrowing tale of a strong group of women fighting for suffrage as they simultaneously struggle to establish their own business. One of the main characters is lesbian, and the oppression faced by women working in the sex trade is a significant sub-plot.

Sweden's *Don't Ever Wipe Tears Without Gloves* gives us a glimpse into gay community in Stockholm during the height of the AIDS crisis. *The Scent of Rain in the Balkans* tells a multi-generational story of a Sephardic Jewish family in Serbia. *Lampedusa* is one of several programs that show the ever-increasing stresses caused in modern Europe from the influx of African and Syrian refugees.

And there's far more than this. With over 2500 hours of programming, MHz allows most of us a chance to find something that meets our personal tastes. Their huge catalog won't give us Latin American or African or Indian or Asian or Pacific Islander programming, which we should still seek out elsewhere, but it does offer these and many other great European shows which are both entertaining and instructive. As LGBTQ viewers, it's always helpful to realize that the local or national culture we live in isn't the only one out there. We can embrace the good we have in our own and try to incorporate aspects from others that can make life better for everyone. Watching these shows will also, I hope, encourage us to tell our own stories, understanding that experiences within *every* culture are worth sharing.

Not Your Grandma's Quilt

From the age of eight, I wanted to be a writer, and now, almost sixty, I've published over 50 books. *The Abominable Gayman, Invasion of the Spirit Snatchers, Gayrabian Nights,* and many more. But there was a brief period in my thirties when, after teaching English for ten years, I went back to school to earn a Biology degree and realized that to do well, I could not afford to lose study time writing more stories about gay Mormons. *Zombies for Jesus* and *Mormon Underwear* would have to wait.

Yet the need to create was as strong as the need to eat, the desire for sexual intimacy. So instead of writing, I found myself learning to quilt. Just as TV commercials warn us that "it's not your father's Buick," I have to say that what I created "wasn't your grandma's quilt."

In addition to the academic challenges I was facing— this was New Orleans, who knew that Nutrition was a thing?—I was also in a committed relationship with a man who was quite ill and in constant pain. We were monogamous, which almost translated to celibacy, sex perhaps three times a year. So my creative outlet also functioned as a sexual release, and many of my designs turned out to be sexually explicit.

Have you ever tried creating a stream of ejaculate out of cloth?

What kind of print is best for illustrating assholes?

First off, I should clarify I had no background in sewing, other than a single embroidery lesson as a child. I did watch my mother and grandmother in rural Mississippi set up quilting frames in the living room and sew a quilt top to a quilt backing, with cotton batting in between, but the top wasn't pieced together with scraps. It was simply two long sections of cloth off a bolt sewn together on a Singer treadle machine. Mom called the end result a homemade quilt, but there was no art and little effort invested. She was a modern woman, only too happy to move away from the farm after graduating high school, her favorite song Petula Clark's "Downtown." But she felt a need to stay connected to her roots, and this seemed easier than milking cows in the suburbs. A few patchwork quilts from before my time were stored in the hallway closet, and I noticed hardly any of the corners matched where the pieces were stitched together. Quilting apparently required talent, and my paternal grandmother hung paint-by-number artwork in her bedroom. I did not have the genes for this.

But I had to deal with my testosterone somehow.

One day while hesitating over a blank sheet of graph paper for a class assignment, I decided to draw a picture. It was crude, all squares, but the subject was recognizable. I realized if I could decide how large I wanted the final quilt top—flaming queen size, naturally—it would be a simple matter to determine the size each individual square needed to be, and I could try quilting this one time and see what happened. My partner had an old Singer treadle, sitting in front of it brought back my mother's wonderful laugh before she died of leukemia, and I pieced together my first quilt top.

Every single corner of every tiny square lined up with the squares next to them. I was dumbfounded. This wasn't even hard.

I began watching quilting shows on PBS, bought some better quilting supplies, and drew more designs. I tried hexagons, and while piecing them wasn't impossible, it was more annoying than satisfying, so I went back to simpler forms and developed a host of pictorial designs using only squares, rectangles, and two different triangles. I finished my degree before advancing to curves and never quilted again after reigniting my passion for writing. I lugged twenty-five quilt tops from apartment to apartment and finally decided I had to find them a better home. Most now reside in ONE Archives, the national LGBTQ archives in Los Angeles.

I designed Rainbow flags with solid colors, Rainbow flags alternating solids with prints, Rainbow flags using denim, Rainbow flags using dyed suede. I designed a Leather Pride flag out of denim, then a quilt with a large pink triangle in the center surrounded by smaller pink triangles, and a Bear quilt using the traditional bear paw pattern but inserting the faces of two hunky "bears" in the center. I put two grooms on top of a wedding cake, pieced together an AIDS ribbon, and put a huge black tornado against a gray sky, bordered with a yellow brick road, poppies, and emeralds. Dorothy's house, flying through the air at forty-five degrees, could be formed easily out of five small triangles.

Then I moved on to a couple of bearded men kissing, their tongues interlocked. I designed and pieced together a quilt of two nude army buddies jacking off, four penises ejaculating toward each other, a quilt showing a dick heading into a man's ass, a dick spurting into the open mouth of yet another bearded man. I designed a quilt top consisting of twenty penises, each in its own block, another quilt featuring rows of men fucking each other in a long train.

When I spent every day in the Animal Behavior lab over Spring Break to catch up on a project, my professor was impressed. "You don't have anything better to do during vacation?" I could hardly tell him my stamina to play with cloth dicks, high as it was, had its limit. So I directed the conversation to a book I'd just discovered, *Biological Exuberance*, detailing the hundreds of other species known to participate in same-sex coupling. At home, I considered designing a quilt depicting gay horses, but even for me, that felt like a step too far. I did take one afternoon off, though, to roam the French Quarter doing some "window shopping." I came up with a design depicting a man's torso wearing a leather harness. That was animal enough for me. But it couldn't be done without going back to hexagons.

Once I was free to write again, I published *Sex among the Saints* and *Sex on the Sabbath* and *Strangers with Benefits*, but during those four stressful years, all I had was Organic Chemistry and quilting to get me through.

Still, not every quilt was sexually explicit. I designed one showing a bookcase, the titles of seminal LGBTQ literature on the spines of the books. I would have needed an embroidery setting to do that effectively, but really, most of these designs were surprisingly easy. The hardest part was resisting fabric sales, only buying what I needed at the time. And, of course, to quilt without unnecessary stress, I quickly discovered the necessity of dedicating an entire room.

And making sure mice didn't get into my fabric stash again.

The only other difficulty with designing and piecing gay quilts is that I didn't often get to share them with other quilters, the majority straight women of a certain age, living in a region not particularly open to the subject matter. To be honest, even some of my gay friends looked at my quilts in horror. But that's the norm for any writer or artist. Many of my friends are no more impressed with my books. *Have Your Cum and Eat It, Too* is not a novel you can pull out at work during a lunch break if you don't want to be called in for a meeting with HR.

One of my other quilts depicted a tractor plowing a field, with gentle hills in the background, which I gave to my dad one Christmas, the only gift I'd ever given him that he appreciated. If I could sew butch quilts, his astonished smile told me, maybe having a gay son wasn't so bad, after all.

That's the beauty of quilting. People can see your work and appreciate it instantly. For a writer, that's extraordinary. We're used to readers investing twenty minutes, two hours, three days reading something we've written before we have a clue if they like it or not. But with visual art, you know immediately. And that's gratifying in a way that writing isn't. It's probably why I've moved on to writing op-eds for newspapers. The time investment for readers is minimal and the reaction is immediate. My essay collections, *Am I My Planet's Keeper?* and *Human Compassion for Beginners*, may not always generate rave reviews, but if no one is ever intrigued or challenged, what's the point of creating anything in the first place?

I find beauty in an ejaculating penis. It doesn't have to *mean* anything.

For those who've long been drawn to homemade quilts but have been worried that quilting is too complicated, that you just don't have any natural talent, I'd encourage you to give it a try. If something doesn't turn out right, you can get a seam ripper and sew the piece again. You can trash a quilt halfway through and start something better. No writer pens a masterpiece on their first attempt, and you're not likely to create an award-winning quilt on your first try. But even "mediocre" homemade quilts are pretty damn charming, whether the corners match up or not. If your dad or sister or cousin never come around to accepting your partner, just give the beloved bigots in your family an attempt that didn't turn out so well.

I no longer have the physical space in my home to do any quilting, and my eyesight has deteriorated over the past couple of decades. But that period of my life when I cranked out design after design to stay sane will always remain an important part of my personal and artistic development. Online, you can find dozens of better quilters who have created far more spectacular LGBTQ quilts. No one needs to remain limited to squares and triangles or even hexagons.

So if you have a little time, a little curiosity, and maybe a little too much testosterone, why not grab a piece of graph paper and see what happens?

Who among us, after all, doesn't want to sleep every night under a comfy five-foot penis ejaculating in a spectacular burst of joy?

Section Four: Race and Bias

Living in a Nun-with-a-Ruler State

"Ugh, I hate spanking students," a friend told me. She was a public-school teacher in Louisiana. "When students are caught breaking a rule, they get to choose who they want to spank them, even if we're not their teacher. I always make sure to hit them with the paddle as hard as I can so they never ask for me again."

As of last year, corporal punishment in public schools was still allowed in 19 states.

Many Americans complain that the U.S. has become a nanny state. "The government" forces us to wear seat belts, bike helmets, and COVID masks. "Sin taxes" are placed on tobacco, alcohol, and sometimes even sugary drinks. We're forced to accept vaccinations, forced to buy auto insurance and healthcare insurance. The government forces workplace safety and minimum wage laws on us. It even passes child labor laws. There are food labeling laws, anti-drug laws, and gun laws.

It's odd that so many who lambast the nanny state for telling them what they can and can't do are the same folks who demand that teachers have paddles. What they want is a nun-with-a-ruler state. This punitive impulse is a driving force behind our bloated military industrial complex and criminal justice system, a massive, secular

Inquisition. We have the largest prison population per capita in the world for our own citizens and the most powerful military in the world to police the rest of the planet.

Sometimes, the two are combined, when our own military, or "federal agents" of unknown classification, with no ID or badges, throw non-violent protesters—our own citizens—into unmarked vans and whisk them away without even telling them why.

When I first began driving, I obeyed every traffic law meticulously. On residential streets, I kept to the required 20 miles per hour. One Sunday on my way to the local Mormon chapel, I saw the stake president's wife in my rearview mirror. Her husband was the highest ecclesiastical authority in all of southeast Louisiana. She was highly respected in her own right. And she was tailgating me.

During Sacrament meeting, she gave me a shout out, saying how impressed she was that I insisted on obeying a rule most people ignored. She'd felt chastened at my example and vowed to recommit herself to always doing the right thing.

The following Sunday, after hesitating for five seconds on my bumper, she zoomed past to hurry on to church. It wasn't as if I was running late, habitually early to everything. She just couldn't be bothered. Some rules simply weren't that important.

And really, she was right. The problem is that in our nun-with-a-ruler state, those same rules *are* important...*if* they apply to someone else.

When police officers stop white folks going five miles over the speed limit, we can expect to hear, "Why are you wasting taxpayer money on something like this? Why don't you go after real criminals? Catch a murderer or rapist! Why are you picking on me over something so trivial?" But we *insist* the police target minorities over the most minor of offenses.

If we can justify an escalation leading to the killing of George Floyd because "he cheated someone out of $20," why are we OK with the medical bills police officers inflict on non-violent protesters? How much will it cost to treat Martin Gugino's brain injury after he was pushed down because an officer was irritated? How much will journalist Linda Tirado pay after a rubber bullet blew her eye apart while she was reporting the news? How much does it cost taxpayers for the inevitable disruption of business and occasional destruction of property in response to continued police brutality? What's the cost to prosecute and imprison people who wouldn't be "criminals" if they hadn't been compelled to protest these unending atrocities?

If it's essential the police stop jaywalkers "for their own protection," why is it that those jaywalkers so often end up injured or dead at the hands of an officer? If the police need to stop someone for not social distancing in an outdoor space or, worse, for wearing a mask in an indoor one, why is it that the offender so often ends up arrested or injured rather than protected? Why do officers threaten to shoot people picking up trash on their own property? Why do they beat and arrest someone sitting on their mother's front porch? What crimes are we even pretending to prevent?

It's clear we're not stopping petty criminals either to protect them or those they might be cheating out of a few dollars. We're punishing them because we see ourselves as nuns, we have rulers in our hands, and we have itchy ruler fingers.

"Oh my God! Look! That guy's getting away with something!"

In the teen drama *The Breakfast Club*, the detention monitor punishes the character played by Judd Nelson with an extra detention for being mouthy. So the student reacts by being mouthy again. And gets another detention. And another. And another. And another. Because the most important thing is for the teacher to work out his frustrations by making the life of a powerless student as miserable as possible.

We accept as a necessary evil police officers injuring or killing someone for having a broken taillight or for selling loose cigarettes. Like my friend teaching in the public schools, we think if we beat our students hard enough, they'll behave themselves in the future or at least won't be *our* problem again. So we assign "demerits" that cost "gum-chewers" hundreds, even thousands, in direct fines or cash bail. We give "detention" to someone smoking a joint or drinking alcohol in public. Not one hour of detention, of course, not even two hours. But ten years. Fifteen years. Rack up enough detentions, and you get "suspended" or "expelled" from society for life.

We've been indoctrinated with a carefully designed catechism to only feel concerned about a specific subset of infractions that impact us. We're OK with fossil fuel companies contaminating groundwater. We're OK with pig farms not sequestering pig feces. We're OK with mining companies not following guidelines to secure their coal ash ponds. We have no problem with industrial farmers using bee-killing pesticides. Guidelines infringe on our rights! We don't need a nanny telling us what we can or can't pollute!

But we call the police on our neighbor for growing wildflowers—weeds!—in her front yard or for "defacing" his own retaining wall with chalk.

Why is it OK for Walmart to cost taxpayers $6 billion a year in food stamps and welfare their underpaid employees still need when we're absolutely committed to a shoplifter who is hurting Walmart to the tune of $6 wearing a scarlet arrest record the rest of his life?

Because Walmart executives have a "God-given right" to make a profit?

Isn't the shoplifter trying to "save money," too?

The double standard is OK, though, because the super-wealthy can lobby Congress to make *their* thefts "legal." It's like only calling the police on a black girl selling lemonade without a license while finding it cute to see a white girl selling lemonade without a license. Unequal justice is more accurately described as injustice.

A classic study with Capuchin monkeys showed that when monkeys in adjacent cages are both given slices of cucumber for performing a task, they're perfectly happy. But when one monkey starts receiving grapes as a reward, the other monkey still being given cucumbers has a fit. IT'S NOT FAIR! As humans, we instinctively recognize this in almost every instance, and it drives us batty when people get away with behavior we don't think they should get away with.

If we reduce our police force, some people will get away with eating a grape they don't deserve!

Aaaggh!

The truth is people already get away with unsanctioned grape-eating. In fact, fewer than half the serious crimes in the U.S. are ever solved. But by golly, we got the damn kid who walked home from the store wearing a mask to keep warm. His crime? Looking "suspicious."

His sentence? The death penalty.

If these abuses were isolated incidents, they'd *still* need to be addressed. But we've all seen enough video to know they are anything but isolated.

If we can appreciate the great sense of injustice *we* experience when other people get away with mostly petty crimes, can we not feel even a *glimmer* of empathy for those whose sense of injustice is sparked because they and their families are killed or imprisoned for crimes others don't even receive a slap on the wrist for?

Perhaps anarchists and libertarians do want to get rid of all policing and regulations. But the rest of us understand we need *some* "law and order." We just want law and order that protects everyone equally, rather than favoring "important" people. We want a system that recognizes that every citizen deserves *all* Constitutional rights, not just some of them, a system that isn't designed to escalate minor incidents routinely, killing us for being deaf and not hearing police commands, arresting us for handing out medical supplies to the homeless, or gassing us with chemical weapons for staying out past our bedtime.

Adults may not need nannies, but a just society needs checks and balances on those with economic and political power to limit their ability to abuse that power. Much of the abuse in our culture is delivered through ruler-smacking "nuns," because who could ever question the sanctity of a convent? It would be like accusing Sister Bertrille of child abuse.

Nowhere in the Bible or Book of Mormon is capitalism established as God's anointed economic system, but you'd be hard pressed to find an American Mormon or other evangelical who doesn't think it's God's law. Policing as we know it didn't exist for most of western civilization, but you'd have difficulty finding an American who doesn't believe "this is the way it's always been" and that our current criminal justice system is the "natural order" of society.

If spanking people as hard as we can is the best policy we can come up with to solve even the pettiest of problems, it's likely because we were spanked ourselves every time we suggested other possibilities.

But we're adults now. We no longer need to accept rules laid down for children. We can question our religious leaders, our teachers, our political and economic leaders, too. It's time to de-ruler some of the abusers in our society wielding the guides as weapons rather than tools and find a more mature and equitable solution.

Preaching to the Goddamn Choir

Speakers and writers often apologize for "preaching to the choir." It's seen as futile or, worse, an exercise at rationalizing and self-justification. But directing our arguments to a group already on "the right side" also helps readers and listeners withstand the gaslighting they receive from other sources. Just as importantly, it acknowledges a basic fact about choirs—not all choir members are on the same page of the hymnal or know how to read music very well.

As a Mormon, I sang every week during Sacrament meeting. Sitting in the pews with our families, we were supposed to follow the chorister's lead, but hardly anyone did. For a while, I also sang in the congregational choir led by the bishop's wife. As a missionary, I sang every morning during Devotional. After I left the Church, I sang in the New Orleans Gay Men's Chorus. One year, we even sang with the opera chorus in a production of *Aida*. People came to these choruses with differing abilities, some able to sight read, some with perfect pitch, some understanding music theory and some not.

I didn't transition from right-wing Republican Mormon to Democratic Socialist simply by walking out of a Church tribunal with my excommunication verdict. What I did leave with was an open mind. Even so, unlearning the lies I'd been taught all my life, and learning new ideas previously kept from me, took a long while, mostly because there was *so much* to learn.

The first several times I heard someone insist it was impossible for *any* white person in America not to be racist, I resisted such an uncomfortable concept. But I couldn't unhear it, and slowly, over many years, I came to understand they were right. They were preaching to folks who already wanted racial justice, but even people who support racial equity aren't all on the same page. We need a music director to guide us or the words overlap, the sound isn't crisp, and no one can understand what we're saying.

I wasn't a proponent of universal healthcare until I heard about it. Only after realizing it was possible, had in fact been practiced in other countries for decades, did I even notice that section in the hymnal existed. I now know several hymns on the topic, some focusing on the need to fully cover dental, vision, and mental healthcare as well. The principles seem obvious now, but we aren't born knowing them. I could laugh when I read the instructions on the side of a box of Corn Flakes in Italy: "Pour in bowl. Add milk. Do not boil." For an Italian, boiling something that at first resembles pasta is the obvious course of action. We can't assume anything. Everything we know we learned somewhere along the way.

I had no reason to advocate for tuition-free college and vocational training till a preacher asked us to sing a hymn about it. With no children of my own, it didn't occur to me that taxpayer-funded childcare and pre-k education were important gospel principles. Thank God for a preacher who gave good sermons on them.

I've long pushed to increase spending for public transportation while many of my fellow choir members with cars haven't given it much thought. They need tenors like me to help them read this hymn's music. Even I needed the alto who helped me understand that we not only need more public transportation but that it must also be fare-free. We both needed the choir director to help us sing in harmony. And we wouldn't even have tackled that difficult hymn in the first place if the pastor hadn't assigned it for an upcoming holiday.

It took a while for me to understand the importance of a woman's right to choose. It's a basic tenet of the left, but I was not on the same page as the pastor or others in the choir for several years, because I didn't forget overnight everything I was taught in my previous religion. Even after joining the new choir, I still needed to hear my new preacher every week, especially because I was no longer browbeaten into doing whatever I was told. I was *expected* to study and act on only what I believed was true. No more "God said it, I believe it, that settles it for me."

As a fully out gay man, I didn't understand trans folks until I saw *The Crying Game.* "I get it now," I thought as I walked out of the theater. Of course, I've heard more sermons since then, sung more hymns, and continued learning more of the doctrine. There are entire universities dedicated to theology. I'm not going to learn everything with only a few homilies a week.

I understand the importance of parables now, that it's easier sometimes to understand a principle or culture if we read or watch a story about them. "Eastern European Jewish culture was lost during the Holocaust" doesn't reach me on an emotional or intellectual level the way reading *In My Father's Court* helps me understand just what was lost. But I can't read every book, learn every relevant principle in the space of six months or even six years. I need to keep singing in the choir and listening to sermons. It's even important for me to hear the same topics over and over so I don't forget what I've already learned. I was once able to sing the Shema perfectly, but I've lost some of my ability because I don't practice it much anymore.

Just as a good Bible class or Torah study can help us get past superficialities, a good minister or priestess can help us learn to ask the right questions.

A true believer in conservation since I was a child, I still needed to hear a few sermons on solar, wind, and wave energy, pointing out both their pros *and* their cons. The religion I follow now is Truth and Compassion, and while some principles may be eternal, our understanding of them is subject to shifting paradigms as we conduct more research. Hydroelectric dams used to sound like a good idea. Not so much anymore. Closing off certain streets to vehicular traffic sounds good for now, as does a modern Conservation Corps to build green energy infrastructure, but I do want to hear more sermons on the subject in the coming months and years. No topic should ever be considered too sacred to discuss publicly, no orthodoxy incontestable. Even as a Mormon, I was taught that we learn "line upon line, precept on precept." I still believe that.

In the public "debate" about climate change, news teams make every effort to present "both sides" equally, despite the preponderance of evidence on one side. Odd that this same effort to appear objective is often missing in the coverage of other matters.

But I wasn't always able to see through the propaganda of "the media" until others showed me how. When a news report airs about riots breaking out during a protest, I watch the video coverage more carefully. Yes, I see tear gas and flash bangs going off, I see people running or fighting the police, but now I question if officers throwing the tear gas and flash bangs are what turned the peaceful protest into the chaos I see onscreen. I no longer accept the news anchor's version of events unquestioningly. "40 people were arrested" no longer means forty people were committing crimes. It literally *only* means they were arrested. Most or perhaps all of those arrested might be innocent.

When a police chief says, "We have to make sure people and property aren't being hurt," I no longer see that as justification for brutality. I think, "An easy way for you to achieve that, Chief, would be to stop abusing people so that they feel they have no choice but to protest." When police chiefs say they can't ban the use of tear gas because they need that option to avoid using excessive force for crowd control, I recognize the spin they're giving to justify their abuse, since tear gas *is* excessive force. Can someone use excessive force to avoid using excessive force?

When I hear news anchors reporting on broken windows or other vandalism, I no longer assume that protesters caused the damage. I've *seen* officers breaking windows. I've *seen* people later identified as white supremacists or other provocateurs destroying property. I don't *discount* the possibility that protesters may have generated some of the destruction, but I recognize that when a news anchor says, "Police report widespread damage to businesses," I'm only hearing one side of the story.

Since these past weeks of protest have been organized in direct response to documented police brutality, broadcasting only police assessment of an event is to support an undeniable conflict of interest. *Of course* police will deflect any personal responsibility. Would you hold a trial where *only* the prosecutor and the witnesses she calls get to speak? Why were no protesters interviewed for the news segment? There were clearly plenty of people to ask.

"Three officers were injured by explosive devices." OK, but who threw those devices? Did an officer deploy them too close to his fellow officers? Did he simply cut himself when he deployed it, causing a minor, self-inflicted injury not caused in any way by protesters? *Maybe* everything being reported is true, but it's definitely not a given, and I recognize how much is implied without being explicitly stated, so that reporters and anchors can pretend impartiality.

The Pope is not infallible. Neither is any preacher I might be singing for. I'm not only free to question the latest sermon I hear from the choir seats—I'm obligated to. And I'm just a chorus member, after all, not a composer. I'm only trying to sing my small part, and I can't do it effectively without continued guidance. Sometimes, even after every single member of the choir has their part down perfectly, the choir director discovers a new arrangement even more beautiful, and we start learning our parts all over again.

Defunding the police or military weren't even on my radar until a few months ago. I'd always thought in terms of small reforms. But now those more sweeping options seem inevitable. When I studied Abraham's attempt to sacrifice Isaac on the altar, I always focused on his dedication to God. Then a rabbi pointed out that Isaac is never shown talking to his father again, and I began to see the story as also conveying something about the human cost of following orders blindly. The test of one's faith isn't to do whatever we're told even if we disagree. It's to question any order that compels us to hurt others for any reason.

As a missionary, I taught "investigators" eight lessons in a specific order before they could be baptized. If someone asked a difficult question, we responded with, "We can answer that question later. First, we need to lay the groundwork so you'll understand the context." Kind of like the classic joke explaining why you can't just tell someone outright their cat died. First, you tell a long story about how it slipped out the door while you were housesitting and climbed up on the roof. It fell while you were trying to rescue it. You brought it to the veterinary clinic, and the vet worked tirelessly to save the cat. After a drawn-out prelude, you can then finally explain that their beloved pet is dead. With the overly extensive background, they're now more prepared to accept the unpleasant news.

As part of the choir, I benefit greatly hearing from the preacher and other choir members. I can learn about Universal Basic Income and re-enfranchising felons who have served their time and legalizing marijuana and polyamory and physician-assisted death. As a Mormon, I was always told to stick to the basics, never to question "the mysteries," but in this new religion, learning and growth never end.

Singing with the choir demands a commitment of both time and energy, but I truly enjoy singing, contributing my small portion to a grand, "joyful noise." One of the best perks of singing about grace and love is getting to hear the pastor week after week. She's *not* wasting her breath.

Please, keep preaching to the choir.

Section Five:
Economic Justice

Taxes Pay for the Nation's Physical, Not Spiritual, Needs

Whenever I discuss poverty with my Mormon family members or former missionary companions, they tell me, "Helping others should only be done out of the goodness of our hearts. The government has no right to *force* us to be kind."

But it's not the government's responsibility to ensure our spiritual growth. The government *is* responsible, however, for ensuring the physical well-being of its citizens.

If we allow people a choice whether or not to help their fellow man, and they choose *not* to, what benefit is that either in building their moral character or in alleviating the suffering of others? It's a lose/lose for everyone.

But if the poor *know* that people aren't just going to throw a handout their way, religious conservatives say, they'll learn responsibility and take care of themselves.

I wonder, though, if a hungry five-year-old is really capable of holding down a good job. Is an eighty-two-year-old? Can homeless parents take care of their homeless children, find a way to wash themselves and their clothes, and travel to job interviews with their kids in tow?

"Well," I hear conservatives say, "my cousin Bob did it! Maria at the office did it!"

That's great. Really. My gay ex-Mormon neighbor climbed Mt. Everest. One of the missionaries I served with in Italy qualified for the Olympics. But exceptional people are just that—exceptions—and everyone, even those who are not extraordinary, deserve housing, healthcare, and food.

Are those who are unemployed because of a pandemic really supposed to pay five months of back rent out of their moral pocketbooks?

If 30 million tenants are evicted because they can't pay such an enormous sum, how does that benefit their landlords? Will the landlords suddenly find 30 million new tenants…willing to pay someone *else's* back rent?

It's another lose/lose for all concerned.

Exactly how moral must one be to afford cancer treatment? How righteous to afford dialysis or insulin or mental healthcare with a minimum wage, "essential" job?

Mormons and other religious conservatives are only too eager to force certain moral decisions on others. They're fine with demanding folks wear clothes in public. They're OK with forcing legal adults to wait an additional three years before they can drink alcohol and requiring those with traditionally untreatable health issues to continue suffering rather than benefit from medical marijuana.

So why do religious conservatives resist being asked to do something that not only helps millions of poor, ill, and uneducated Americans but also improves the success of the nation as a whole?

I regularly hear from conservatives, "All you people want is to take, take, take!"

But doesn't that imply what conservatives want is to "keep, keep, keep"?

Does that latter behavior get conservatives points in heaven? Do Mormons get their "calling and election made sure" by leaving others to suffer simply because they aren't extraordinary?

Sure, religious conservatives donate to religious institutions, and those in turn give some financial assistance back to the community. But they also get to pick and choose who receives their generosity. That's their right, of course.

But it doesn't help everyone. And the government is responsible for *all* its citizens.

When I hear religious conservatives praise morality-promoting austerity programs, I can't help but wonder if any of *them* ever received assistance from their parents with tuition. Any help getting a car? Housing? Free babysitting?

If these folks don't feel sinful and weak for accepting help, why would such a moral stain exist if someone *else* receives help from a friend? Or from the entire community?

If we can all pitch in and fund bomber jets and killer drones without feeling morally compromised, why are we so resistant to spending even a fraction of that to provide food or post-secondary education or healthcare to our own citizens? To our neighbors? Why does *that* destroy our character?

If the military is worthy of our forced benevolence because it ensures our physical well-being, surely these other essentials are worthy as well.

Families have their responsibilities. Religions have theirs. As do individuals.

But the government has responsibilities of its own that shouldn't depend on the conflicting caprices of its citizens.

It is the personal responsibility of each of us to support the government in accomplishing its task of ensuring the physical well-being of everyone it governs.

Not only support, but demand.

With Compassion Like This, Who Needs Cruelty?

"Hardship builds character. If we gave you a living wage just for working a full-time job, you wouldn't push yourself to improve."

"You won't retain what you learn unless you pay for it yourself. If you know you'll be in debt for the next thirty years, you'll study harder."

"You'll never grow to become a compassionate human being if we interfere by relieving your misery."

It's heartwarming to see how deeply those who insist our lives be as miserable as possible care for us.

When we're dying of painful, terminal illnesses and ask for the right to take Death with Dignity medications, these religiously motivated humanitarians say, "Only God has the right to end your suffering."

And yet these same, faithful souls seem to have no issue with taking over another of God's tasks—making *sure* we're miserable. If only God can *ease* our suffering, why isn't it God's task alone to *make* us suffer?

Nice of a loving God to let us share in that. Or of his followers to insist on it.

Too often, the righteously motivated go out of their way to codify our suffering into law. We make protesting fossil fuel pipelines that threaten our land and water a felony. We attack peaceful protesters with tasers and pepper spray for speaking out against police brutality. We protect corporations putting their employees in dangerous work environments from liability.

In every way possible, we strive to make the lives of "the masses" as miserable as we legally can, and if those ungrateful peasants dare to complain about "injustice," we do everything in our power to make sure they suffer even more.

Of course, the only way we can live with ourselves for treating other humans so brutally is to lie—to them and to ourselves—that we're doing them a favor. "You'll thank me for this later." And if those thanks never come? It just proves that the recipients of our "kindness" are ungrateful wretches who need to suffer a bit longer to learn the right lessons.

But it's not only a matter of making others suffer. By doing so, we make ourselves suffer, too.

When right-wing, middle-class religious conservatives find themselves living in cities with high crimes rates, when they're worried about their children associating with low-class, ignorant, "dangerous" kids, their suffering is needless as well.

We don't want to shop at a store where "unsavory" folks are shoplifting? We don't want to struggle finding an employee who can do basic math? We don't want to drive through a neighborhood where homes are boarded up or have paint peeling from the siding?

The truth that can set us free is that we don't need to. Instead of spending trillions on war, we could spend mere billions on war and the rest helping our fellow citizens. Instead of allowing CEOs to avoid taxes, we require them to pay their fair share. If we're not intruding on God's will by making middle-class folks pay, why would it be intruding on God's will to have the upper classes pay, too? If they suffer as a result, aren't we "helping" them improve their character? Won't they thank us later?

And if demanding that corporations and the wealthy pay their fair share of taxes is "bad" because it somehow ends up hurting "the poor," hasn't that been what we insist our goal is all along? Won't the poor benefit from the suffering they endure because the wealthy are paying taxes?

When we help others in our community, help others across our country, then our entire community benefits, our whole nation is lifted. Why is this fundamental truth missing from the "prosperity gospel"?

We can be capitalists and still not demand people live in abject poverty. Even the rather nasty, anti-Semitic Henry Ford understood that *he'd* be better off if his employees earned enough money to buy his products.

An uneducated, untrained workforce is a national security threat. We can divert a fraction of our military budget to fund tuition-free college and vocational training and become a stronger, safer nation as a result.

The climate crisis is real, not an ideological construct. But if we want people to band together to address it, make whatever sacrifices might be necessary, we can't abandon them to unemployment and poverty and eviction. No one can worry about climate disaster hurting their children twenty years from now when they can't put food on the table this week.

No one can focus on climate when they can't pay their medical bills.

We want mothers to stay at home taking care of the kids? If we really think this work is so valuable, let's pay stay-at-home parents a stipend.

Of course, some countries already offer their citizens a Universal Basic Income. And they remain capitalist countries. The options to *either* have capitalism along with extreme poverty and suffering *or* soul-destroying "socialism" is a false choice.

Considering, though, how profit has consistently been the motivation for corporations to keep the dangers of tobacco, fossil fuels, and PFAS (the chemicals in non-stick and stain-resistant products) away from consumers so they could rake in exorbitant profits while poisoning people and the planet, a truly God-fearing person might at least *consider* the failings of capitalism.

"They'll thank us later for making them suffer…and making their children suffer…and making their grandchildren suffer." Those who can't see through that lie yet need to understand that many millions of us do.

If it's "not right to act like God" when it comes to compassion, why is it OK to do so when it comes to punishment and "teaching people a lesson"?

Perhaps the most important question to ask ourselves is this: If we're so intimidated by the task of helping our fellow man that we don't even want to begin, that we *want* to leave it all up to God, then what is it we think we're supposed to do to love our neighbor as ourselves?

It's *got* to be more than just feeling satisfied that their suffering is for their own good.

And if it *is* a sin to ease someone's suffering, maybe we ought to consider sinning a bit more. After all, God can always make us suffer for it later if he chooses.

Loaded Questions, Logical Fallacies, and the Presumptive Close Keep Us from Claiming Our Rights

"Senator, when did you stop beating your wife?"

We learned in freshman English different types of logical fallacies and unfair techniques used both in political argument and sales, really any effort at "persuading" others to go along with a desired outcome.

The question above, of course, assumes that the senator *has* been beating his or her wife and that the only detail still uncertain is whether or not the behavior has stopped. It's a loaded question.

A similar method we learned was to close a sales pitch with something like, "So did you want the five-year warranty or the seven-year warranty?" when the customer hasn't yet agreed to either. By framing the question as if the major decision has already been made, and that the customer need now only choose minor adjustments, the sales associate has a better chance at closing the sale.

It's easy for those on the left to disentangle the deceptive and manipulative messaging of conservatives, but many of us still have difficulty recognizing when "our side" uses the same methods.

Republican opponent will win!"

But are your policy positions significantly better than
those of your opponents? The fact that I don't want a right-
wing candidate to win doesn't automatically mean I want
you.

Supposedly, any candidate even a millimeter to the left
of a conservative must be supported at all costs, but since
most of us have limited funds, we have the option of
considering a third or a fourth or a fifth possibility. We
can't fund every campaign in every race in the country. So
we give to candidates in specific races whose policies *will*
serve the public.

If there are left-leaning millionaires out there with
money to burn, *they* can donate to the candidate who is
only minimally to the left of the conservative. *We* can
donate to progressive groups that then start preparing a
new slate of primary challengers and other candidates for
the next election.

So let's rephrase that manipulative fundraising
request. Instead of "Rush a donation to me today or my
terrible Republican opponent will win!" how about "Rush
progressive policy changes to your website today or you
won't raise the money you need!"

We are not bound by the wording candidates and
elected officials use to frame the issues.

The same is true of "liberal" news anchors, who limit
airtime to progressives and then editorialize using GOP

talking points against them, misrepresenting facts and framing issues to slant both how elected officials and the public perceive them.

"Single-payer healthcare will cost trillions of dollars! How will you ever pay for that?"

Healthcare *already* costs trillions of dollars. Cost projections for single-payer healthcare show that we can instead *save* money. "A recent study shows that the U.S. could save two trillion dollars over ten years by adopting a single-payer system. Why do you *oppose* saving money, when doing so *also* guarantees healthcare for every American?"

What's important is not to let others force us into a framework that doesn't allow us to answer the questions that need to be asked.

We keep hearing conservatives say that Trump was "well within his rights" to bring dozens of lawsuits challenging the 2020 election results, that 147 members of Congress were "well within their rights" to challenge the Electoral College certification. Those are actions, they insist, protected by the Constitution. "You can't say the President and these members of Congress are insurrectionists when they're doing what's allowed in the Constitution."

Constitutional scholars who make such claims, however, are being dishonest or, at best, disingenuous.

Sometimes, an either/or scenario *isn't* a logical fallacy.

After all, conducting a trial by jury is "well within" the rights afforded by the Constitution. But does that mean it's lawful for people to intimidate members of a jury? That witness tampering is legal? Is obstructing justice acceptable as long as it's done during a jury trial? Is it "well within the rights" of attorneys to present false evidence? Can perjury be condoned because trials are allowed under the Constitution? It's OK for attorneys to call on a mob to storm the courtroom and terrorize or kill the witnesses?

When Trump and his enablers lied again and again, insisting they had "proof" but presenting none, they weren't "well within their rights." They were attempting to overthrow the results of an election and prevent the peaceful transfer of power. The Constitution does *not* grant that right to anyone.

Loaded questions, logical fallacies, and the presumptive close keep us from claiming rights which we *do* have, a denial preventing our realization of a just society.

We must learn to recognize when we're being manipulated—by *anyone* of any political persuasion—and reclaim the framing so that we aren't always on the defensive but can instead take down the façades of those opposing progress and justice.

"Hey, DNC," we might ask, "when did you stop beating your voters?"

Nag a Ram: Anagrams for Human Rights

In fundraising email after fundraising email, Democratic candidates say things like, "People need healthcare! Please donate to my campaign!" Even newly-elected officials send these fundraising requests, always asking for contributions toward their *next* campaign years down the line. The problem is that most of these "leaders" still haven't come out publicly in support of Medicare for All or any other type of universal healthcare program.

But "Please rush a donation now!"

Their emails are non sequiturs. Acknowledging a need while promising not to address it isn't the incentive conservative Democratic politicians seem to think it is.

I reply to such requests with, "It's not complicated. We need universal healthcare. It's a basic human right."

I can't even encourage friends to donate in my place. "Hey! Give money to this guy! He promises not to listen to his constituents!"

I keep saying the same things over and over, either to the candidates, my elected representatives, or my conservative Democratic friends. Am I wasting my breath? Am I beating my head against a brick wall?

If demanding that public servants serve the public is a waste of time, keeping silent while millions suffer is a waste of life.

Only a handful of issues are truly "essential," so I'm limited to how many points I can make. I worry my essays and conversations are no more than anagrams. I keep rearranging the issues and solutions, hoping that one arrangement finally makes sense to someone.

A friend of mine, a small business owner, complains that Democrats don't care about her, that they keep raising her taxes while providing taxpayer-funded services to the poor.

She's not entirely wrong. The problem is that she thinks denying even limited services to the poor would help her business grow. She's been trained by leaders of both major parties and by corporate media to believe only two options exist. It never occurs to her that we could demand the wealthy pay higher taxes, that we require corporations pay their fair share, too.

In my city, public transportation throughout the downtown sector was completely free to passengers for many years. Then budget cuts required that folks begin paying. When the pandemic struck, fares were abandoned altogether, downtown and throughout the county. No one was even allowed to board through the front door.

Homeless people began riding more often, sleeping or seeking shelter from the rain. And I began hearing, "We need to start charging fares again or we'll just be transporting homeless people around all day."

That's only a danger because we refuse to address homelessness itself. We price the poor out of living within city limits, and then we place another heavy financial burden (and time constraint) on them by making them pay for long commutes to and from work. And we can't remedy that injustice against the working class because we keep refusing to address the greater injustice of *why* homeless people are riding the bus competing for seats.

Of course, transit has to be financed by *someone*. We're simply channeled to believe this can only be accomplished by charging low-wage workers.

One of my bosses, who operated a business in a low-income neighborhood, complained regularly about homeless people urinating and defecating in the parking lot behind his store. Yet he also complained whenever I allowed a homeless person to use the bathroom our paying customers used. Short of incarcerating half a million or more homeless people, or executing them all, we have no other choice but to put up with their urine and excrement.

Unless, of course, we choose to address natural biological functions.

What would the cost of long-term incarceration for half a million people be compared to the cost of establishing public toilets across the country and paying employees to clean them? What's the cost of leaving human waste throughout our cities? What's the impact on business revenue when customers won't shop in certain areas because we ensure those neighborhoods will be filthy and repulsive?

What's the toll on the mental health of every citizen when we live in a society that treats fellow humans like shit?

We don't like folks shoplifting, but what is a menstruating woman supposed to do if she can't earn a living wage? If she can barely pay her rent, she's not going to be able to afford sanitary napkins or tampons.

In Sunday School, I was taught to keep the Sabbath day holy. We weren't supposed to work unless we "had" to. Cows needed milking every day, so milking one's cows was acceptable. If your ox fell in the ditch, you didn't have to wait until Monday to pull him out.

The sin, my teacher explained, was in spending all day Saturday pushing the ox *into* the ditch.

The system isn't broken. It's been designed this way. When people are forced to concentrate all their energy on getting one more meal on the table, they aren't in a position to demand a bathroom, to demand an EpiPen. We're so consumed with literal survival that we don't have the time, energy, or funds necessary to demand accountability of our elected officials.

That's the way they want it. Our desperation serves them, offers them security.

Some desperately poor coworkers and friends of mine do donate to candidates who say, "People need healthcare!"

"He gets us," they tell me.

"Yes," I agree. "He's got you. Right where he wants you." A better term for this fundraising technique might be "extortion."

Power is never granted freely, not even by the politicians "on our side." If we want basic human rights, for us *and* our fellow citizens, we can't keep taking "Later" for an answer.

I'll continue sending these anagrams to the politicians who petition me, and I encourage my friends to send anagrams, too.

TOED GNU VIP

NUDE GOV TIP

DEVOUT PING

GOD PET UNIV

Or simply, "DON'T GIVE UP!"

Discount Human Rights

Time and again, Democratic candidates claiming to be progressives refuse to push for the bold changes we need. Instead of universal healthcare, they work to "reduce" prescription prices and make healthcare "affordable." Instead of guaranteeing a college education or vocational training to every adult who wants it, they make it a "priority" to offer "assistance" or to "lower tuition costs." Instead of emergency action on climate, they want to "help" people start "reducing" emissions, with a net zero goal somewhere far past the date reaching it might permit us to avert catastrophe.

We don't need discount human rights. No cheap substitutes. We demand acid-free attention, not ground pulp respect that quickly becomes brittle and breaks apart.

These counterfeit progressives say, "Something is better than nothing, right?" "Change takes time." "We have to represent our entire constituency, not just the radicals."

Imagine an apartment complex housing thirty units catching fire. When the fire engines arrive, the building manager comes out and says, "Lucia on the third floor is afraid of water because her aunt tried to drown her when she was a child. So you can't use water anywhere on the right side of the building above the second floor."

Maybe that "constituent" does want this kind of accommodation. But is it a practical way to put out the fire? Everyone suffers because we give in to an unreasonable demand. Sure, *some* people like raking in outrageous profits from fossil fuels but tailoring our response to serve 800 people while ignoring 8 billion is not a sustainable approach.

What if the owner of the apartment complex forbids the fire department from responding to calls altogether? Neighbors pitch in and toss pots of water against the building because they want to help. Something is better than nothing, right?

Will even one apartment in that building be saved with this level of "something"?

Homeless encampments have sprung up all over my city in recent years. Every few months, city workers are dispatched to "clean up" the encampments. This means throwing away everything possible and forcing the homeless outcasts to start setting up camp somewhere else. An eternal wandering in the desert, an unending diaspora. The displaced homeless must now scrounge for new tents, new cardboard, new everything and start over. A couple of months later, the new area is "cleaned," the destitute robbed again of what little they have, as they are cast out into yet another part of the city to start the whole, horrible process all over again.

Homelessness is not "solved" by such an approach. It's not even alleviated.

"But they're ruining the neighborhood!"

That may be. But hating homeless people won't shower their bodies or wash their clothes. Refusing to talk to them won't help. Tossing their belongings won't, either. And refusing to empty their trash cans only makes the problem worse.

You know what helps? *Help.*

"Allowing" someone to rummage through garbage to survive is a bargain basement human right. Even if our sole concern were to help middle-class residents, we can achieve that only by helping the poorest members of our community as well.

When I lived in New Orleans, my family in outlying communities refused to visit. It was too scary, too dangerous. "Ooh," my aunt told me once, "you ride the *bus*? Ooh."

Public schools receiving discount funding according to their zip code simply weren't up to the task of providing the educational opportunities necessary to raise vast stretches of the city out of poverty. Inner-city residents suffered as a result. Middle-class and upper-class residents of the city suffered, too, with high crime rates and a huge unskilled, barely employable workforce. Even my suburban and small-town relatives suffered because they missed all the cultural opportunities New Orleans offered those brave enough to ride the bus or—gasp—walk along the sidewalk.

Everyone benefits when we all receive the healthcare we need. Everyone benefits when we aren't spending hundreds of billions to cover increasingly destructive hurricanes and wildfires. Everyone benefits when we have a well-educated, well-trained workforce. Everyone benefits when every worker is paid a living wage.

Half measures, incremental steps, platitudes, and even sincerity aren't enough. When we talk about the right to free speech, we don't say, "We're only going to let ten people from each community ask the senator a question this year."

Yet this is the way we parse out other human rights. We offer cheap Blue Light Specials of tear gas and pepper spray against our own citizens. We offer consumers "a deal" by putting them out of work and then evicting them when they can't pay their rent.

There ain't no such thing as a free lunch. And there's no such thing as a partial human right.

Or did I misread the Bill of Rights? Are we only guaranteed 3/5 of each right?

Our concept of human rights changes over time, evolves. Businesses that don't grow with the times fail. So do governments. Civilizations, too. As enlightened as America's Founding Fathers might have been in relation to what came before, they weren't gods. We don't have to stop progressing past the years 1776 or 1787.

"Constitutional originalist" sounds impressive. Pure. Untainted. But if we're talking "intent," the authors and signers of the Declaration of Independence and the Constitution "intended" to allow continued enslavement of other human beings and deny women the right to vote. Let's not Make America Barbaric Again.

An unrecognized right still exists, just as a virus does, even if it can't be seen with the naked eye.

We need universal healthcare.

We need tuition-free college and vocational training.

We need government-funded childcare and full funding of all public schools.

We need housing.

We need a living wage.

We need our elected representatives to treat the climate crisis like the emergency it is, not trivialize it with empty gestures: "I raked up all the dry brush from a third of an acre in the Sierras. Paradise should be set for fire season now."

Discounting our rights only costs us more in suffering, ignorance, poverty, crime, sickness, and death.

We don't like skimping on the quality of our food or shoes. We don't like cutting corners on the reliability of our phones and televisions. We don't like pirated DVDs and handbags.

Pinching pennies with human rights will get us bootleg criminal justice contaminated with methanol, Social Security sanitizer contaminated with 1-propanol.

America broke away from England to recognize rights that had been denied. But we still can't seem to escape our cultural baggage. We must stop being "penny wise and pound foolish" and grant our people Grade A, Premium, Choice, First-Class human rights.

It's Risky to Nominate a Democratic Socialist: It's Also Risky Not To

Every day, pundits worry that it would be risky to nominate a Democratic Socialist to run in the general presidential election. They are 100% right. What they fail to note, of course, is that it's also risky to run a centrist. *Any* Democratic nominee is going to face an uphill battle. So let's choose the candidate with the best policies and fight as hard as we can to elect that candidate.

In 2016, Democrats *did* nominate a moderate. It didn't go so well. If people want to blame progressives or the Green Party or Putin or the Electoral College or anything else, the fact remains that every type of election interference from four years ago still exists today.

What if we nominate Warren? Trump and the GOP will attack her for having "claimed to be an Indian." What if we nominate Klobuchar? The attack will be that she's an "activist lawyer" or, conversely, that she prosecuted innocent black defendants.

Biden is "low energy" and sometimes stutters. No matter how inappropriate it is to mock him for his occasional trouble speaking, a president who mocks disabled reporters and POWs won't have any problem doing so. Will it subconsciously diminish Biden in the minds of voters? We don't know. But it's risky. And it's hardly Biden's only weak spot.

Buttigieg is gay. Would Trump suggest that having a First Gentleman would make the U.S. look bad? Of course he would. Just as he'd complain about Bloomberg "buying the election." Or Steyer having no experience in office. Pundits seem to have missed that Trump is a hypocrite *and* that his hypocrisy means little to his supporters. He'll use a Pee Wee Herman "I know you are but what am I?" attack on any opponent, no matter how ridiculous it looks to rational Democrats. And that approach works for him. Have we not been paying attention?

It wasn't just centrist Hillary Clinton who lost a bid for the presidency. Al Gore lost, too. So did Walter Mondale. And Adlai Stevenson. And John Kerry. And Michael Dukakis. And more. Yes, sometimes running a centrist is a winning strategy. But sometimes, it's not. It's risky. Just like running a Democratic Socialist.

The question is whether it's easier to rally a potential voter behind "We will guarantee you healthcare and a college education and a living wage" or "We can't really give you anything you need, but we can get rid of Trump."

Get rid of Trump! Yes! We want that!

But it's a false dilemma. A centrist can't guarantee he or she can win against Trump any more than a Democratic Socialist can. If it was guaranteed, we wouldn't need the election in the first place. It's risky to choose *either* option.

So we must add other factors to our decision. And those other factors *must* include policy proposals.

Would Republicans have a hard time working with a Democratic Socialist? Undoubtedly. But are we under any illusion they'll eagerly work with *any* other Democratic president? If I remember correctly, GOP lawmakers weren't all that keen to work with Obama.

If a centrist's only significant argument is that they'll stop the country from deteriorating further under Trump, it's also true that a Democratic Socialist will do the same. We get that from either type of nominee.

If the stakes are so high that we need to go with the safest bet, the bland status quo of past centrists is hardly justifiable as that safe wager. We are in a time of crisis. Even without Trump in office, economic inequality has been growing for decades. Americans have come to understand that universal healthcare, something guaranteed in the rest of the industrialized world, is a right. What's risky is ignoring the tangible, physical needs of the people casting their ballots.

Most voters believe the science proving the climate emergency. They aren't going to be pacified with candidates who accept donations from fossil fuel corporations. A promise to "gradually" and "pragmatically" approach a crisis the majority understand must be addressed immediately is more than risky. It's foolhardy.

I want a woman president. I also want a Latino. And an Asian. One black president was hardly enough. I'd also like a Jew. And maybe an atheist. As a gay man, I'd certainly like to see a gay president.

But what we need more than any of that is a candidate with policies that will help us all. Medicare for All isn't negotiable. Neither is tuition-free college or vocational training. Or a Green New Deal. *Polls show that the majority of voters want these things.*

If it's a purity test to demand that a candidate support a woman's right to choose, we as an electorate have the right to demand other non-negotiables as well.

Is that risky? Of course it is. But it's even riskier not to.

Democratic Voters Have a New Level of Expectation

The novel coronavirus outbreak is shining a light on what all but corporate Democrats—and truthfully, even quite a few of them—have known for some time. Unjustifiable inequality in healthcare, educational opportunity, housing, and income are damaging not only to "the poor" but to the entire country as well. As a former Republican who became a Democrat who became a Democratic Socialist, I've seen this shift to the left among a growing number of friends and acquaintances over the past decade. Some moderates still worry about progressives demanding too much from their candidates, but what was acceptable in the past is no longer sufficient. It wasn't true *before* COVID-19 cases started surging across the country, but elite Democratic leaders and corporate media can no longer prevent everyone from seeing the evidence right in front of them. Voters have a new level of expectation.

I'd already earned three English degrees before I started working on a degree in Biology. While some of my Biology Lab 1001 classmates struggled, I routinely earned a 95 or 100 on every quiz. After nine years of college classes, I knew perfectly well how to be a good student.

All I had to do was review my notes three times before class and I was set.

Or so I thought.

Life changed when I enrolled in a sophomore level Cell and Molecular Physiology class. I found myself muddling along with B's until mid-term, when I finally started earning A's again. Despite all my previous coursework, much of it even at the graduate level, it turned out I still needed to up my game. Meeting with my professor in her office, I confessed, "It took a while for me to adjust to this new level of expectation."

She nodded knowingly.

In my senior level Biochemistry, I filled out almost 500 index cards per exam, drawing molecules and complicated molecular pathways. For that one class, I learned what would have equaled the coursework for three or four junior level classes.

Moderate Democrats criticize progressives for having a litmus or purity test. "It's your way or the highway," they complain. "You need to be flexible and get what you can. If you insist on all or nothing, you'll get nothing. And you'll take the rest of us down with you."

I don't know a single progressive, though, who is insisting on *everything*. Even countries with universal healthcare and tuition-free college still have plenty of problems. We're not expecting Utopia. But we do expect more than freshman or sophomore level rights.

Rights, by definition, aren't a luxury. Was there a financial cost to ending slavery? Was there a cost to gaining suffrage for women? To guaranteeing marriage equality? The specific dollar figure isn't the important question. All people deserve to be free, whether there is a small cost, a moderate cost, or any other level of cost. The truth is, when *all* costs are taken into account, it's always less expensive to "give" people basic human rights.

Too many moderates seem to have only one non-negotiable demand—that the candidate be a Democrat. When I began my Biology degree, I hadn't taken a math class since high school and needed to enroll in two remedial classes to catch up before I could tackle Physics or Chemistry. My professors didn't lower their standards. I had to rise to meet the requirements.

A remedial level of non-negotiables isn't a viable path for a Democratic candidate anymore.

But my recent conversation with a moderate gay friend didn't go well. "Would you vote for a Democrat who didn't support marriage equality?"

"We already have marriage equality."

"You didn't answer my question."

"Well, I voted for Obama before he endorsed marriage equality."

"You still haven't answered my question. Would you support a candidate *now* who spoke against same-sex marriage?"

My friend still refused to answer, so I moved on.

"Would you support a candidate who was against a woman's right to choose?"

"If my only other option was a Republican, then yes."

"And if you have other Democratic candidates who *do* support a woman's autonomy over her own body?"

My friend frowned.

"Would you vote for a Democrat who wanted to eliminate Social Security and Medicare?" I went on.

"No Democrat is going to move backward."

"Would you vote for a Democrat who refused to stop separating children from their parents? Would you vote for a Democrat who felt racial justice had already been achieved and needed no further effort? Would you vote for a Democrat who threatened to pull out of NATO? Who sold off our national parks? Who didn't believe the disabled deserved rights?"

The fact is we *all* have non-negotiables when making decisions on which candidate to support.

Healthcare is a human right. Tuition-free college and vocational training are non-negotiable. Aggressive, immediate action on the climate crisis is non-negotiable. The coronavirus shows the futility of allowing elite political leaders or corporate media to pretend these "unrealistic demands" are only items on a wish list. They are quite literally the difference between life and death, both for individuals *and* for the nation as a whole.

That's especially true for the Democratic Party, which cannot expect to pass Local or General Election 2020 if they don't meet a higher level of expectation.

My Biochemistry professor didn't grade on a curve. If we answered a complicated essay question with 95% accuracy, we didn't get any points at all for that answer. Our democracy isn't in kindergarten any longer. We're not high school students. We're not freshmen college students. We are the teachers, and we can no longer accept candidates unable to comprehend that casually reviewing their notes three times before an exam isn't going to earn them an A this time.

Voters aren't giving candidates honorary degrees. If Democratic candidates across the country want a passing grade, they must adjust to a new level of expectation.

Progressives Must Accept It's OK to be Hated

Progressives give in again and again because they don't want to hold up aid, they don't want to prevent at least some token effort at solving a problem, they don't want people to think they're mean and selfish. They definitely don't want to be hated. But this constant fear makes them powerless. You can never be the alpha if you're always lying on your back exposing your stomach to show submission. Progressives need to accept that if they hope to accomplish anything meaningful, they must be willing to be hated.

"But we're the good guys!" I hear progressives say. "We're trying to make the world a better place! How can we do that if people hate us?"

First of all, we need to accept the reality that people *already* hate us. Those on the right do, without a doubt. But a great many moderate Democrats do as well. Don't you hear it in the disdain with which they dismiss our reluctance to support Biden as the Democratic nominee? "You say there's not much difference between Republicans and Democrats? Well, I say there's not much difference between a progressive who won't vote for Biden and an idiot who votes for Trump." I was told that by one of my longtime "friends." She has no trouble being hated, takes it as a badge of honor.

While I wonder about her strategy of bringing progressives to her side by calling them idiots, I do think she's onto something by not being "nice" all the time. Krystal Ball, on her show "Rising," finally helped me understand the power we can wield if we are willing to be hated. If we cede all our power by placating bullies, either those on the right or those in the middle, we end up pleasing no one. The right still hates us. The corporate centrists see us as their "bitches," and progressives are disappointed we've failed them yet again.

Most of us on the far left *are* nice people. When we make people mad, when we upset them, we are usually humble enough to question our behavior. Are we in fact doing something wrong? We don't want to be bullies ourselves. But this constant second-guessing and waffling robs us of the power to accomplish anything meaningful. Those times we *are* wrong, we need to adjust our ideas. But that shouldn't be 99% of the time.

I was the only Mormon in my Baptist High School. As a senior, I came in second place for Most Popular. Frankly, I was surprised even to do that well. I was more disappointed to come in second for Best Christian Example. I really wanted to be first in that.

I did, though, end up as Most Courteous on the senior superlatives page of our yearbook.

Sally Field's Oscar acceptance speech—"You *like* me! You really, really like me!"—resonated with the audience because we understand how desperately everyone wants to be liked.

But did the Tea Party worry about being liked or did they worry about getting legislation passed that they wanted? Do Republicans worry about not offending Democrats? Does Trump worry about looking "mean"?

We certainly don't need to be cruel just for the sake of cruelty. We don't need to be cruel at all. But we do need to stand firm on what is right, *even if* other political leaders on "our" side hate us for it.

Even if we alienate a family member or lose a friend.

As a Mormon, I was always taught that family was the highest good in life. David O. McKay, one of our prophets, claimed that "No other success can compensate for failure in the home."

Several of my closest family members haven't spoken to me in years because I won't back down on gay rights. That was painful. But I got the fuck over it and moved on.

We must be willing to be abandoned even by the people we love *if* we expect to champion the rights of the poor, the sick, the oppressed, and anyone else crushed by right-wing Republicans *and* corporate Democrats.

Every day on the news, I watch anchors and pundits wail about how awful Trump is. They always ask some form of the question, "Can we finally now agree that Trump is bad?" Hey, guys, you proved that *three years ago* and *every day* since then. Can we *please* shift the conversation to solutions?

And stop telling me the solution is to give in to moderate Democrats who don't get us what we need. "Trump won't get it for us, so you have to vote for us!" But they won't get it for us, either. How do we know? Because we see the evidence every day. Moderate candidates won't even put Medicare for All on their platform. Or tuition-free college. Or a Green New Deal.

To be nice to their corporate donors. They certainly aren't being nice to their prospective constituents.

And those already in office aren't failing to pass good pandemic aid packages because more people on the other side are voting against their wishes. *They're* voting against anything good in those bills, too.

To be nice. To placate. To not look like bullies. To not be the bad guys holding up aid.

And the result?

They hold up aid and any meaningful legislation to improve our lives.

I imagine my moderate political friends singing the Mormon hymn, "There is beauty all around when there's love at home."

With love like this, who needs hate?

Just like my Mormon family, moderate Democrats tell us every day, "If you just repent and come back into the fold, we'll like you again."

Yeah, don't do me any favors.

You want my financial contribution to your campaign? You want my vote? You want my power? Then don't tell me to roll over and offer you my throat. Give me something worth my money, my vote, my power.

Because if you don't, you've proven you already hate me anyway.

Lotteries Are Essential…but They Shouldn't Be

State and national lotteries are still open during the pandemic, considered essential businesses. And they *are* essential. The problem is they *shouldn't* be. The lottery website asks players not to make a special trip just to purchase a ticket, to buy tickets only when they are part of a planned visit to the grocery store or gas station. But that's rather like a television ad for alcohol showing people partying to excess and concluding with, "Please drink responsibly."

We all know that human psychology is complex, that people still smoke despite the Surgeon General's warning on every package of cigarettes, despite commercials showing throat cancer survivors puffing out of a hole carved into their neck.

I've been at church gatherings where someone will offer a benediction over the refreshment table. "Heavenly Father, we ask thee to bless this food that it will strengthen and nourish our bodies." Then everyone digs into the potato chips and doughnuts.

Lotteries take advantage of our deeply ingrained ability to ignore the truth. So do politicians.

I continue to buy lottery tickets during the pandemic, even knowing I'm risking my health and the health of my husband. Why do I behave so irresponsibly? Why am I so cavalier about the danger to myself and others?

I do it because I'm desperate.

Even before the pandemic, I was barely getting by with two part-time jobs paying only slightly above minimum wage. At the age of 59, I'm still paying down my student loan. I have no siding on one wall of my house. I'm on public transportation. I've lost one of my jobs to the virus and may lose the other. I'm still eight years away from Social Security, assuming the program hasn't been completely gutted by then.

So I walk twenty-five minutes to the closest grocery to buy lottery tickets and another twenty-five minutes back.

Even as I acknowledge my difficult circumstances, I think of the undocumented workers who can't get any assistance at all. I think of asylum-seekers trapped in conditions that will kill a third of them once the virus starts sweeping through detention centers. I think of the millions of prisoners with convictions for non-violent offenses who are sitting ducks in confinement. I think about how those released early have nowhere to go. I think of all the other homeless folks in the U.S.

Most of the people demanding we "reopen the economy" don't have a death wish. Some, of course, are deluded by the false information they receive from right-wing corporate media. But others simply realize the government isn't going to help them. Their anger, however, is misplaced. What they should be demanding is universal healthcare, fair wages, a universal basic income, dismissal of student loans, and higher taxes on the rich. When we see 22 million new unemployment claims simultaneously with a steep rise in the stock market, we know that a "successful economy" does not include us.

I'm not the only person buying lottery tickets, but we try to stay six feet apart in line.

My sister, an LPN at a nursing home, is out with a suspected case of COVID-19. Suspected, not confirmed, because of the difficulty in obtaining a test. She gets no health insurance from her employer, hasn't seen a doctor in *years*. Even the ACA hasn't been any help, as she's never been able to afford the policies offered. It was cheaper for her to pay the tax penalty and *not* get coverage for her money.

In the movie *Logan's Run*, almost every citizen is killed when they reach the age of thirty. A few people, though, have a fighting chance, if they participate in a game that has them flying up through the air trying to reach the lone prize. As spectators watch, the contestants are zapped to death, one by one. During the course of the film, the hero discovers to his dismay that *no one* ever wins.

The regional lottery office one town over from me is closed until the pandemic is over. If I do somehow end up with a winning ticket, I'll need to take public transportation to the state capitol to claim it.

In 1991, when Klansman David Duke ran for governor of Louisiana, former governor Edwin Edwards, known for his corruption, saw a chance at re-election. One of the unofficial slogans of the campaign was, "Vote for the crook. It's important."

Edwards, who loved his trips to Las Vegas, never wasted a single dollar on the lottery. He understood gambling well enough to realize what the odds of winning were.

One of the courses that drove up my student loan balance was Statistics. I understand the odds, too.

But there is another lottery tonight, and I've already bought a ticket.

Maybe *this* time, I'll win. My money troubles will be over, and I'll finally be free to retire immediately.

To spend my remaining years a witness to the horrors caused by an economic and political system that feasts on the misery of the poor.

Unless we become as relentless in changing the world as a novel coronavirus.

Please Contact Me When You Have a Platform Worth Supporting

Because I donate to progressive causes and candidates, I end up on a great many email lists for other candidates I've never heard of. One of them emailed me recently, informing me he was progressive and asking for my financial support. His email didn't reveal much of his agenda—the assumption was that I'd just hand over my money simply because he claimed to be one of the good guys. But when I checked him out online, I discovered that despite good policy proposals on climate, he did not support universal healthcare. I emailed back and explained that while I found him overall to be better than most Democratic candidates across the country, my finances were limited, so I could only donate to those who met all of my minimum requirements. His lack of support for a national health program was a deal breaker.

I'd been polite in my email, and the candidate replied in a similarly non-confrontational manner. "I believe in offering my constituents a choice," he said, "so I think Medicare-for-All-Who-Want-It is the best solution."

He's not the only candidate to say something along these lines. It *sounds* reasonable but it really isn't. I grew up in a right-to-work state in a religiously and politically conservative family. As a teen, when I heard about right-to-work legislation on the news during dinner one evening, I announced emphatically, "No one should be *forced* to join a union."

My father, a contractor who'd spent the previous twenty years building houses, wasn't impressed. "If you don't belong to a union," he told me, "you have less job security and you make less money. And if everyone else on your job site belongs to a union, whatever benefits you do get are because *they're* paying all the dues while *you* contribute nothing."

During Obama's presidency, I saw the same dynamic in the debate over the individual mandate for the Affordable Care Act. The difference there was that the premium was 30% of my monthly income, hardly "affordable." A law can't successfully force someone to hand over money they can't earn. The system was designed to fail.

Which is a similar problem facing the post office. Congress has deliberately made it impossible for the US Postal Service to succeed. It *had* been one of the most successful government programs in history. But if we sabotage it, of *course* it won't function adequately. Then pro-corporate politicians can say, "See? The private sector can do this better."

It's not uncommon for a failing company to hire a new CEO "to turn things around." All too often, though, the company's failure by this point is unavoidable. So a woman or an ethnic minority is hired for the position, and when the company does finally go under, everyone can say, "See? Women [or blacks or Latinxs or Asians or whoever] just aren't good at business."

Britain's National Health Service was one of the best in the world until recently, when politicians began turning pieces of it over to private corporations. *Now* it's become less efficient. All a set up so that pro-corporate leaders can say, "See? Socialized medicine is a failure."

Even Medicare for All in the U.S. would struggle as long as pharmaceutical companies and medical supply companies remain for profit.

We have no problem awarding billions in bailouts to corporation after corporation. Money for FedEx but not for the post office. Money for drug companies but not for a national health program. "That would be an abuse of taxpayer dollars!"

Odd how our "principles" only kick in when politicians can no longer direct funds to their corporate donors.

Many CEOs accept bailout money and then continue firing hundreds, even thousands, of employees. As Robert Reich regularly points out, "Billionaires aren't going to save us."

Private prisons give corporate owners an incentive to encourage long sentences for minor offenses, even to label some behaviors criminal that shouldn't be. The way some unethical dentists keep finding "issues" with a patient's teeth, performing one unnecessary procedure after another to keep the money coming in. The way an untrustworthy mechanic can keep finding "problems" with our car engine. The way weapon manufacturers are incentivized to promote war.

Democrats like to point out every conflict of interest President Trump or Mitch McConnell or other Republican leader has.

But when profit is the goal, every system, as well as every leader in it, has a built-in conflict of interest.

Is capitalism too big to fail? Perhaps. But it's definitely too profit driven to succeed.

Money is power, and corporations have most of it. The challenges we face to reach economic, social, and climate justice are overwhelming. The least we can do—and often the most—is direct our limited funds and energy *only* to those candidates and causes which meet the minimum requirements, and demand accountability when we do.

I emailed the politician who'd contacted me one last time. I didn't want to sound snarky, and I suspected my note would be interpreted in that tone, but I meant my comment sincerely. "When you finally have a platform worth supporting, please contact me again."

Zero is Not an Increment

Moderation is a virtue. Compromise signals maturity. Reasonable people vote for centrists. Working across the aisle is the only way to pass legislation in Washington. In a fiercely divided Congress, incremental change is the best we can hope for. But to all those who complain that progressives are asking too much too quickly, I'd like to point out that zero is not an increment.

The claim of success would be false, even if incremental change was in fact taking place. But all that "realistic" Democrats have gained us lately are *fewer* Supreme Court judges, *fewer* district court judges, *fewer* appellate court judges.

"It's not our fault!"

And yet Democrats blast Republicans for never taking responsibility for anything.

The last Democratic president ordered *more* deportations than his predecessor. In the first two years of Obama's presidency, Democrats controlled both houses of Congress as well as the Oval Office. And yet couldn't even muster the courage to put single-payer healthcare up for a vote. Virginia is currently led by a Democratic governor, a Democratic House, and a Democratic Senate, giving Dems the power to do virtually anything they want. Yet, according to Oxfam, Virginia is still 51st out of 50 states plus the District of Columbia in the arena of workers' rights.

51st place out of 51. The incremental advance there is zero, as it is in far too many places on far too many issues.

Remember the episode of *I Love Lucy* when Lucy and Ethel bottle their own salad dressing? They tell Ricky and Fred they're making money, but it turns out their profit is just three cents per jar, "and that three cents goes to Caroline Appleby" for getting them an advertising spot at her husband's television station.

"But we'll make it up in volume," Lucy declares bravely.

Basic math quiz: what is 3,957 times zero?

I remember a particularly dry summer in Mississippi during my early teens, when everyone's corn crop was shriveling in the heat. One afternoon, I told my dad excitedly, "It's raining!"

He looked outside and gave a dismissive grunt. "Not enough to do any good."

I didn't understand. Surely, a little water was better than no water, right? But my father was correct. While technically a five-minute light drizzle isn't "nothing," its effect *is*. "Something" has to mean more than a trace, it has to mean "something that changes the outcome in a meaningful way." .034 inches of progress isn't "zero" but it may as well be.

When criticizing Republican distortions of the truth, Democrats like to quote Nazi propagandist Joseph Goebbels—"If you tell a lie big enough and keep repeating it, people will eventually come to believe it." Those terrible, dishonest Republicans.

And yet Democrats keep telling those of us on the left a Big Lie as well: "Keep voting for us and we'll finally get you what you want. I know it doesn't look like it right now, but you have to look at the bigger picture. We're working behind the scenes for you. Just trust us a little longer. Only 10 or 20 years. It's not forever. We're really trying. Have patience, and little by little, we'll save you. As long as you keep the faith and stop complaining. Complaining will destroy everything we've accomplished so far."

Explaining that what we need isn't what we've been given is apparently more powerful than Democratic legislation, stronger even than Republican opposition. Those idiots who demand the capacity to pay their rent are the real reason we don't have more progress.

Odd that complaining about Democratic inaction is bad but complaining about progressive goals is just fine.

The federal minimum wage, adjusted for inflation, is lower now than 50 years ago. From 1968 through 1974, the minimum wage was $1.60 an hour, which as of January 2020 was equivalent to $11.65. The actual minimum wage in January 2020 was just $7.25. That's -$4.40. I suppose a negative number is an increment, if we don't mind going in the wrong direction.

But has there really been *no* progress in the past several decades? Of course there has. A black man can now become president. While a jogger can still be shot just for being black. Lesbians can get married. While a woman impregnated by a rapist is still forced to bear the child. *And* grant the father partial custody.

When an energy revolution is needed immediately to limit greenhouse gases to levels that keep large swaths of the planet even marginally inhabitable, an incremental approach to lower emissions by 2050 just isn't going to cut it.

No human society will ever be perfect. But it's not unreasonable to expect more in the U.S. than we currently have. Other nations have had universal healthcare for 70 years. Some have had tuition-free college for decades as well. If Democrats still can't provide these basic needs for us after all this time, do even measurable increments really matter?

Might that be the reason more and more people give up and vote for Independents and Democratic Socialists and the Green Party and, when profoundly desperate, even someone like Trump?

The claim at election time is always the same. We're facing an emergency. We need to get the terrible Republicans out first and *then* we can worry about moving forward later. But a rallying cry of "We can't do anything just yet but we honestly intend to one day" isn't effective, even *if* it were true. And, finally, by small increments over many years, our faith in empty promises has grown too large to ignore.

If Democrats want to lead, they must take us where we actually need to go.

Zip Ties and Apron Strings

In December of 2015, I started giving away some of my prized possessions. I didn't have many, mind you. But I loved reading middle grade literature: Enola Holmes, Sherlock's younger sister, who solves mysteries he can't; Theodosia Throckmorton with a gift for seeing which ancient Egyptian artifacts are cursed; Laura Ingalls recording the life of townspeople trapped inside during an interminable winter.

A few times each year, a young mother in my neighborhood stopped by with her young daughter to gift folks on our block with treats, and I decided to offer her the books I would no longer need. I didn't tell her I was planning to commit suicide. I simply said I no longer had space for them and thought her daughter might enjoy them.

The woman became convinced I was stalking her and refused to speak with me again.

The possibility that my actions could be so deeply misconstrued had never occurred to me. Frankly, I'd only been worried she might see through this well-known suicidal behavior and try to save me.

But we neither act nor react in a vacuum. Men are often predators and women are often targets. As a cashier, when I'm enjoying what I think is a casual chat with a female customer, I can tell the moment she begins to suspect the interaction isn't innocent. "Well, I guess I need to get back to my *husband*," she'll say.

"Oh, yes," I'll reply, hoping to relieve her worry, "I need to stop by the store for *my* husband on the way home." It never relieves her worry.

Even when women know I'm gay, they are often unable to keep themselves from seeing me primarily as a man, a leering, disgusting predator. To be fair, viewing unfamiliar men this way probably serves them well most of the time. But I was deeply hurt at a moment when I was already at my most vulnerable.

But when all was said and done, divesting myself of my favorite juvenile literature—my neighbor did take most of the books—still ended up a positive experience. I felt unburdened. Inanimate "things" can be comforting, but they also bestow an unavoidable obligation. They must be protected, preserved, dealt with. How do I make sure my books aren't damaged by sunlight coming through the window? What happens to that Val St. Lambert art deco vase during an earthquake? How would I ever manage to transport my wooden dinosaur carvings if I had to move to another home? What if the bank foreclosed and threw all of these precious items onto the curb? Even if I was unable to keep them myself, I didn't want them to just be thrown away. I had to protect this mini-Dresden from enemy bombs.

My personal library used to contain *thousands* of books. It's now down to seventy. In a perfect world, I'd have an entire room devoted just to the books I love.

But it's not a perfect world. It's not even a world, at least for the time being, where I can walk to the library and select another book to read.

When my printer died a couple of years ago, I chose not to buy another. For the few items I needed on paper, I could go to one of two neighborhood libraries or to FedEx.

Unless, of course, there's a pandemic.

Which brings us to healthcare, inexplicably tied to our employer, trapping us to our workplace because it's too dangerous to lose coverage when we leave.

In December of 2015 I was contemplating suicide for a variety of reasons, but the most immediate was a deep loathing for my job. I'd somehow ended up in a mortgage department processing equity loans. The workload was overwhelming, support from management was minimal, and more was being demanded of me every day.

The morning I woke up and thought, without hyperbole, "I'd rather die than go to the office today," I knew I had to quit.

I was HIV positive, with diabetes. I couldn't remain even moderately healthy without medical care. But what good is insurance, I asked myself, if I jump in front of a train? With only a few hours of guaranteed counseling, "coverage" was an anchor dragging me down, not a life preserver keeping me afloat. The need for income, obviously, was its own quicksand. The more my husband and I struggled, the more desperate our situation became. We might now lose our home. But when I was faced with the choice of daily misery to remain under a roof or daily misery from homelessness, I chose None of the Above.

My self-esteem was tied to my employment as well. It's difficult to feel good about yourself if you can't hold down a decent job. If you're not tough enough to stick it out. If you're not capable enough to overcome obstacles.

So I went from feeling suicidal to feeling even lower.

Yes, things *can* get worse. But it's almost always because we openly participate in our own bondage, believing that emotional and financial S&M is the sophisticated way to live. By definition, this behavior can't be an outlier if it's the norm.

We're tied to the desire for our parents' approval. My father was never impressed when I taught at a university. He wasn't impressed when I worked in a bookstore or at the library. For a few brief years, he was proud as I returned to school for a Biology degree so I could apply to medical school.

But when I didn't get in after several interviews, he went back to believing I was never going to do anything "worthwhile." And even if I didn't fully agree with his assessment, I was tied to it. Because mainstream society is also tied to it.

In the book, *The Object of My Affection*, the kindergarten teacher doesn't want to become a principal. He wants to remain a kindergarten teacher. But in the film version, he *must* become a principal for the movie to have a happy ending. To remain in such a lowly position would make the hero a loser.

As a bank teller, I wasn't permitted to feel content doing transactions at the window. My manager counted it against me in evaluations if I wasn't actively trying to "advance" to "the platform." The point of being a teller, he felt, was to use the position as a steppingstone to success—becoming a loan officer.

But I didn't want to become a loan officer. I wanted to be a good teller. And so I was marked down.

The Cowardly Lion in *The Wizard of Oz* boasts that he can fight with one hand tied behind his back.

Most of us must fight throughout our entire lives while handcuffed.

Decades after I left the Mormon Church, I married another ex-Mormon. When I met his brother, a former bishop and then a temple worker, I understood the high status he possessed. And still, when I learned he'd chosen not to serve a mission when he was nineteen, I was disappointed to find myself judging him.

We spend a lifetime learning familial, religious, and cultural expectations. And we're tied to them even when we don't want to be.

"You've lost some weight," I said to a friend I hadn't seen in a while. "You look good."

I'd meant it as a compliment, but aren't the accompanying unspoken words, "You sure looked awful before"?

Our self-esteem is tied to our appearance. It's tied to our education, to our income, to the prestige of our job or position in our religious community.

My previous husband was financially bound to a city he wanted desperately to leave. But his need to stay in a tenure-track position kept him trapped and too depressed to think of a way out.

One of my early boyfriends was rather "unfortunate looking," according to one of my friends, who assured me repeatedly, "You can do so much better." This friend, quite attractive himself, had been with his partner, also attractive, for many years. And his attractive partner beat him regularly. He'd been to the emergency room on more than one occasion and had the stitches to prove it. But he also "had his standards" and would never be caught dead with a man who looked like my boyfriend.

He was perfectly willing, of course, to be caught dead by his abusive "catch."

A close friend, this one another Mormon, was trapped in a marriage to someone she seemed at times to loathe. Her husband cheated on her on countless occasions and was obnoxious under the best of circumstances. When I asked during my last visit how he was doing, she said, in utter disgust, "He's still alive, isn't he?"

And yet she could not allow herself to consider divorce because that would mean she couldn't be with him for all eternity as a reward for her successful temple marriage. A temple marriage she somehow believed would be rewarded on Judgment Day despite her husband's repeated infidelity. A reward I couldn't fathom her wanting in the first place.

One of my husband's aunts clung desperately to life despite increasing health problems because she didn't want to be forced into her deceased husband's company again, her choice either to be trapped in an ailing body or bound in the afterlife to a man she despised. Prison now or prison later but always prison.

We're tied to the party line in politics, not allowed to dissent. Mitt Romney can be the Republican presidential nominee one day and shunned even by other Republican Mormons later for saying anything critical of President Trump. And Democrats can criticize Republicans for not allowing dissent while then lambasting any Democrat who steps out of line.

My second partner suffered chronic, debilitating pain and was prescribed OxyContin, but he had a difficult time getting what he needed. I read several articles and learned that opioids were only addictive if you took them when you weren't in pain. If you *were* in pain, the opioids addressed the pain instead of triggering addiction. I became an advocate for my partner, trying to get him the pain medication he needed. I didn't understand why he needed to shift to methadone.

Only years later did I learn that pharmaceutical companies had deliberately misled us.

It's mortifying to have been wrong about something that destroyed so many lives.

Almost all of us are bound by the need to save face. When new information is available and there's the possibility we must adapt our position, we often can't because we're afraid of admitting we were ever wrong to begin with. It's not enough to say, "When I know more, I make better decisions." We can't apologize for hurting others. We can't be happy we're progressing from bad to less bad to better to even better. We'll look weak, we'll look fickle, we'll look stupid. We'll have to accept that we may have spent twenty years defending something that in the end is indefensible.

A woman who left the Mormon Church in her sixties reported on Reddit that she felt those sixty years of life had been stolen from her. Some people would rather not have ten or twenty final years free of delusion. Better not to acknowledge the loss at all, to actively choose to remain deluded. Like chaining yourself in the basement, or inside Plato's Cave.

We're tied to the way things have "always" been done, unable to grasp that capitalism is no more a natural or God-given system than feudalism before it. We're trapped by either/or thinking. We either "reopen the economy and kill people" or "save lives and destroy the economy," unable to process any of the dozen other possibilities, some of which we can see in action in other countries leading the way. We either "hold people responsible" or "let them get away with anything." We see ourselves as either successes or failures, saints or sinners, supporters either of good government or oppressive policies. Those are the only options.

Worst of all, we allow all of these various cords to bind us to permanent submission against any action to save ourselves. We let ourselves be afraid of demanding healthcare as a human right. We let ourselves be convinced the only two options are corporate healthcare or single-payer, with socialized medicine too far-fetched to consider. We let ourselves be afraid to speak against the consensus of our peers. We let hundreds, thousands, millions of other people, most of whom we'll never meet, scare us away from being happy with our unimportant jobs and extra pounds and our children's books and our unstylish clothes.

We're trapped by our unrealistic dreams and by the inappropriate dreams of others. We're trapped by the fear of pursuing our possibilities. We're trapped by the pain of trying to achieve them and falling short.

But the pain isn't inevitable.

For years, I believed myself to be the most despicable being possible because my Church told me so. Yet when I came out and learned the history, science, and culture behind gay life, I no longer felt that anguish. It wasn't that

I chose not to feel it anymore. The pain disappeared on its own once I realized its origin was entirely artificial.

I remember Lucy helping Ricky audition for his role as Don Juan. When she keeps hogging the audition so *she* can be discovered, she's tied to a bench to keep her in her place. And when she repeats her line, "Oh, that I could cut these ties that bind me!" she delivers it with real feeling.

Lucy Ricardo never makes it in Hollywood.

But we all love her anyway.

Perhaps we should begin to sing a love song to ourselves at least once a day. Make it our personal opening credit.

We've heard it a thousand times. "Be true to yourself." "Find your passion." "Dance like nobody's watching." The problem, of course, is that we only hear this counsel from "successful" people, which undercuts the message. Oprah found her passion, didn't she? So if I follow that advice...

No, we can't all be Oprah. And we shouldn't want to be. She does a great job of that by herself.

Let's do what *we* want to do with *our* lives. Hopefully, it's something that helps the world and doesn't hurt. But we can't *make* ourselves "be good" if it's not something we really want. On a note card taped to the top of my computer screen, I've written in bold letters, "Happiness isn't the goal. Lead a meaningful life." We must trust ourselves to make reasonably good decisions and be willing to adjust them as we go along. And if that doesn't bring us everything we ever wanted, that *has* to be OK.

Because "success" can never be anything more than making a handful of pivotal decisions in the course of an entire lifetime, whatever their outcome.

Let's make a good decision today.

Section Six:
Cultural Divide

America, We Need to Talk

Have you ever received a "Needs Improvement" on your report card? Ever struggled to advance from "Meets Expectations" on a performance review at work to an "Exceeds Expectations"? Ever had a "come to Jesus" moment with a spouse or wayward teen?

Recognizing weaknesses, occasional bad behavior, or undeveloped skills isn't an attack. It's a necessary step toward improvement.

Those on the political right seem to feel that any criticism of America means those making the criticism hate our country. Conservatives experience incredible rage and disgust in response. But critics aren't criticizing to show superiority. We have plenty of room for improvement as well. We're pointing out problems because those problems exist, they hurt millions of our fellow Americans, and something *can* be done to rectify the problems.

As long as we don't live in denial.

Like a friend of mine whose father was excommunicated from The Church of Jesus Christ of Latter-day Saints right before her temple wedding. "Don't tell me why," she said. "I don't want to know."

I heard something similar from a coworker about her husband. "Bob keeps saying 'we need to talk,' but I know he'll tell me he's having an affair, and I can't bear to hear it."

When I was a Mormon missionary, my companion and I held "Companion Inventory" once a week to discuss issues we might have with one another, so our resentment wouldn't fester.

Couples experiencing problems in their marriage often seek out marriage counseling. Families look for family counseling. Does that mean we hate our spouse and kids? Or just that we want to make our marriage and family stronger?

When a conservative Christian leader or politician is caught having an affair, he is readily forgiven by his followers and supporters if he apologizes. Most of us believe, after all, in repentance.

But if America betrays its people and denies it, or rationalizes it, or tries to weasel out of it, that's not repentance.

If America betrays its ideals, admits it happened, but then doesn't apologize, that's not repentance.

If America betrays its people and ideals and does apologize but then doesn't make restitution to the extent possible, that's not repentance, either. It's certainly not redemption.

In the LDS Church, folks who commit semi-serious sins are subject to what used to be called "disfellowship." (Now they call it "formal membership restrictions.") Once they pass probation and prove themselves worthy again (by admitting their sin, vowing not to commit it again, and making appropriate restitution for whatever they've done), they're welcomed back into full fellowship.

Mormons call the Church tribunal a "court of love." Even when a member is excommunicated for serious sin, we're told the act of expulsion is done out of genuine care and consideration. We're helping our loved ones take the difficult steps to make amends and become the better people we know they can be.

So why does it mean I hate America if I point out a flaw or two that needs attention?

What many essential workers, people of color, and folks on the left feel is that we've become the person our spouse *doesn't* want to go to marriage counseling with. Our spouse doesn't even want a divorce. Our spouse simply wants to kill us and bury us in the desert. We're the unwanted toddlers drowned in the bathtub.

We read what our conservative friends and family post on Facebook. We see the news reports of militias planning to attack us and hear the deafening silence of your refusal to condemn such behavior. For years now, realizing we were always the ones reaching out, we wait for you to initiate contact, with an email or phone call or holiday card that shows you even care we're still alive.

When we see you cheering people and policies that demonize us, when you post memes about putting us in prison, when you see us shot or arrested for peacefully protesting—pointing out one or two of America's legitimate flaws—and say with a shrug that we got what we deserve, we understand something that you don't.

We know what it feels like to have our loved ones wish us dead.

America, we need to talk.

But please don't panic. Let's all take a deep breath. It's going to be OK. We love you, and together, despite your flaws *and* ours, we can find a way to work all of this out.

The Radical Right Is America's Ammonium Nitrate

We've seen the horrific images from Beirut after a warehouse full of ammonium nitrate exploded. Brides were blown off their feet, windows came crashing in on children, ceilings collapsed on top of priests, 300,000 residents transformed into homeless wanderers in an instant. All because greedy and corrupt leaders left 2700 tons of volatile material open to catastrophic failure if the right conditions were ever met.

The same forces in the U.S. are systematically transforming a large portion of our own populace into explosive material that may lay waste to our nation.

We've grown up with stories of shapeshifting werewolves and vampires. We watch movies like *Ladyhawke* and *The X-Men*, read books like *How to Walk Like a Man* and *Wild Seed. Calvin and Hobbes* always had their transmogrifier handy.

We're less familiar with people transforming themselves into explosives.

That's essentially what the 9/11 hijackers did, what the Las Vegas concert shooter did. It's what Trump and other desperate GOP leaders are doing to a large segment of the conservative right.

We're informed of "isolated" incidents, shooters targeting a Black Bible study or a synagogue or Sikh worshipers. We hear of "random" attacks on LGBTQ folks, on Native Americans, against Muslims. We hear of "lone wolves" murdering Latinx shoppers at Wal-Mart. And we see a regular stream of "bad apple" police shootings of unarmed Black men, women, and children.

The fuse, though, is the growing support for such behavior from the increasingly radicalized right.

We are subjected to a deliberate, undisguised effort to transfer wealth to the top 1%, pitting the rest of us against each other, creating the most fundamental ingredient for the explosion. We're subjected to a deliberate attack on vital infrastructure, a deliberate refusal to act on the climate crisis, a deliberate plan to disenfranchise more and more voters. Access to human rights becomes a game of musical chairs where the losers lose everything.

We see reporters physically attacked by right-wing politicians, their supporters, and the police. We hear praise for murderous vigilantes from the president himself, from other elected officials, from the police, right-wing pundits, and our right-wing relatives on social media.

Conservative candidates label Democratic leaders sociopaths. They call for the killing of gays and gay allies. They declare those on the left cannibals and child traffickers. The description they give of everyone not a far-right conservative is so repulsive that anyone who believes that description can't help but want to take action.

One spark under just the right conditions and our country will explode. It was just such a spark that set off WWI in Sarajevo, just such a spark that set of Kristallnacht in Germany, just such a spark at Ft. Sumter that set off civil war in the U.S.

Too many on the right envy the bomb from the movie *Speed*, which Dennis Hopper describes as needing to explode if it is to fully embody its nature, its essence. Too many *want* to be triggered, *want* to be ignited, so that the subsequent murders won't really be their fault.

They willingly allow themselves to be convinced they are doing "God's work." They see themselves wielding the "sword of God." There's a reason that those who sing, "Onward, Christian Soldiers" now call themselves members of "Patriot Prayer." "Saturday's Warriors" itch to embark on a religious rampage like the Crusaders of the Middle Ages who slaughtered "infidels" by the hundreds of thousands.

Christian conservatives rail against "Sharia law" while working to enact "God's law." They sneer at radicals who kill in the name of "Allah" but have itchy trigger fingers of their own, desperate for the opportunity to kill in the name of "God."

They wait for a sign to grant them permission. And guaranteed absolution, so they can sin without guilt.

Maybe even get bonus points on Judgment Day.

It's like getting a free pass to cheat on your husband or wife. It goes against the morals they've been taught their entire lives, but they want it so desperately they deliberately choose leaders they know will provide it.

Trump supporters are flooding phone lines now in Oregon claiming "antifa" are setting the wildfires ravaging the state. There appears to be no lie too low, no behavior so base, that the far right won't use it to attack their fellow man.

The ammonium nitrate is all around us, in every city and state, susceptible to the right conditions virtually anywhere. Even if we manage to avoid a cataclysmic explosion in the coming months, chances are the amount of hazardous material will only continue to increase over the next few years. Yet a pre-emptive strike again these radicals would only add to the danger of a massive detonation now.

The only thing we can do at this point is vote flamethrowers out of office. And that doesn't just mean voting against Trump as if he is the only arsonist. It means voting against *all* flamethrowers and *for* "firefighters" on school boards and city councils, in county government and state legislatures. It means being willing to run ourselves.

It means boycotting companies that financially support flamethrowers, no matter how inconvenient. It means filing lawsuits and pushing for positive change, even if it's time-consuming and expensive. It means no longer arguing with far-right members of our family who have willfully chosen never to be persuaded by facts. It means we stop fanning the flames ourselves.

We don't take the bait, we don't make that easy dig. We de-escalate while not giving in.

Because if we can't remove the source of heat from the unstable material, we'll be responsible—not equally but substantially—for the ensuing tragedy as well.

Yet we do still one more thing. We make contingency plans in case the ammonium nitrate does indeed explode. Because those perfect conditions only have to be met once for that huge warehouse to be transformed into a mushroom cloud which could envelop the entire nation.

From "We'll Hide You" to "We'll Turn You In": Sowing Hatred and Division in the "United" States

I've had a valid U.S. passport for forty years. When enhanced driver's licenses became available, I paid extra for one. As a gay man who'd lost a friend to gay bashing, as someone who worshiped alongside a Holocaust survivor, I always knew there might come a time when I had to flee. I was going to be ready.

It's disappointing to realize now that I'm not making it out. I've grown old, gained weight, have diabetes, trouble with my knees. I'm all too aware I can't even run if I participate in a rally and the police start indiscriminately attacking non-violent protesters. A similarly worried friend told me he's making methodical plans to emigrate overseas in the next three years.

I think he's too late.

If my husband and I make it through the next three or four months, *maybe* we have a chance. I encouraged my friend to continue with his careful plans but to understand that "moving" or "emigrating" might not be options. His only choice might be escaping as a refugee.

I don't have that option.

I write lots of leftist political essays. I write "radical" stories of LGBTQ ex-Mormons. I'm a secular humanist. I'm poor.

I'm not getting out.

When Obama won the U.S. presidency back in 2008, Whoopi Goldberg said something like, "All my life I've had my suitcase packed." She understood she wasn't safe in America. But after Obama won, she said, "I feel I can finally put my suitcase down."

Even then, my first thought was, "Well, *I* don't feel like that."

After my excommunication from the Mormon Church, I converted to Judaism. But before my rabbi would approve my conversion, he asked one last question. "Are you ready to face another Holocaust if it comes to that?"

"Anyone coming for you," I answered, "will be coming for me, anyway, but yes, I'm ready."

He then smiled and brushed away my comment like he was swatting a fly. "This is America. It won't happen here."

I remember thinking, "Does this guy understand human nature at all?" He was (and is) a great guy, but I've long understood the absolute worst could happen here.

Because for many, *many* people, it already has.

I volunteered two years of my life as a Mormon missionary in Rome, and I've made sure over the past forty years to keep my Italian in workable shape. I studied Spanish and French, even Russian and Hebrew. I watched European shows on MHz to help me understand other cultures and practice my language skills.

I was determined to be ready if I ever needed to get out. And I've studied enough Holocaust literature to understand that one can't wait 'til the very last second.

As the scientist played by Ian Holm in *The Day After Tomorrow* says, "I'm afraid that time has come and gone, my friend."

It's *hard* to move even across town or to a different state, much less to another country. Getting a decent job in the best of times is a challenge. So even though I've wanted to leave for several years now, it simply wasn't feasible. I've watched as things grew more and more tense, as the risk of roundups or "vigilante" mass killings grew stronger. Still, my refugee bag was ready to grab at a moment's notice if necessary.

But I waited too long.

I listen to my Mormon friends and family say the most horrific things about gays, about Blacks, about Democrats, about—gasp!—Democratic Socialists. Years ago, two extended family members assured me that if the government ever came for "the gays," they'd hide me.

Reading their posts now, I realize they'd be among the first to turn people like me in. I really don't know, of course. They no longer speak to me.

As a teenager, I asked my father, a contractor, if one day he'd build a house for me with a hidden room so I could hide Jews if I needed to.

But now I need a haven of my own.

I hope enough rational, decent people vote Trump out in November that I'll still have a fighting chance at life and liberty in my native country. I hope that the insurrection Roger Stone and other Trump supporters are calling for if Trump loses doesn't happen.

I hope that after the election, refugees at our southern border are released from their cages and prisons, that we stop mass incarceration of our own citizens. I hope that Americans get the healthcare and education they deserve. But so many Democratic leaders are against these things as well.

Still, I hope, and I write, and I rally, and I vote…while I can.

Because I'm here to stay, whether those who hate me like it or not. And, really, whether *I* like it or not, either.

Vote Shaming Doesn't Work, but if Reasoning Doesn't Either, What's Left?

Several months ago, while Bernie Sanders was still in the lead during the primaries, a sarcastic friend of mine on FB lambasted everyone still voting for him. Smart, ethical folks, he insisted, would only vote for someone with a legitimate chance of winning the nomination. This friend sneered at stupid purity voters who weren't being realistic. They were the fools, he whined, responsible for putting Trump in office in the first place. I decided that such a dismissive attitude wasn't helpful. Clicking Unfriend eliminated at least that one bit of daily negativity from my life.

As it turned out, the DNC and prominent Democratic leaders did make sure that Biden became the nominee, despite being the worst or possibly second worst candidate in the primary. Perhaps no one else ever had a chance in the first place, corporate media equally as guilty in pushing the worst of the corporate candidates. Just as Hillary Clinton was appointed, so was Joe Biden.

What makes supporting the resultant nominee more distressing is his refusal to shift to the left on even one of the most vital issues. Biden is more interested in persuading Republican voters than progressive voters, feeling we have no choice but to cast our ballot for him.

But we do have a choice. Several of my friends flat out refuse to vote for Biden. And they're not alone.

Mind you, none of them would have voted for Sanders, either, considering him too far to the right as well.

But even now, with the West Coast ablaze, Biden continues to support fracking. He thinks his decision to push for mass incarceration years ago was the right one. His running mate, Kamala Harris, refuses to admit any errors from her own harsh history in criminal justice. I don't want *any* leader who can never learn from their mistakes, who cannot hold him or herself accountable for their decisions, who can never process additional evidence, who is announcing publicly and proudly upfront they will never adapt to evolving conditions. They know *all* the answers now, and nothing anyone can say or do will ever change their mind.

Really, that attitude is supposed to be an asset?

Of course, this is the same behavior that Never Democrats are engaged in.

I asked one of my Never Democrat friends if there was anything at all Trump could do that would lead her to vote for the Democratic nominee. She said no. Democrats support corporations. They oppress workers. She correctly pointed out that in the midst of a pandemic and economic crisis that leaves the unemployed without healthcare, Democrats still won't support single-payer healthcare. She doesn't believe Democrats will ever solve any of our problems. *No matter what* Trump says or does, she and her friends will NEVER vote for a Democrat, under any condition. Ever.

A great many articles online rail about the evil of "voting for the lesser evil," but how can it be *better* to guarantee that the greater evil stays in office? If Trump announced that once elected for a second term, he would round up all LGBTQ folks, sterilize all Blacks and Latinx, execute Native Americans, would it still be better never to vote for a Democrat? If there *is* a line that could be crossed that would spark a change in voting strategy for Never Democrats, where do they draw that line?

And for God's sake, why don't they think it's been crossed yet?

Never Democrats claim that the DNC and their media accomplices are tricking us into believing we have no choice, but even independent, alternative media clearly document the atrocities Trump and his appointees have committed and their plans to commit even more.

Emmanuel Macron pushes some oppressive policies. But isn't he ANY better than Viktor Orbàn?

Angela Merkel is sorely lacking as a leader. But isn't she ANY better than Kim Jong-un?

Alexandria Ocasio-Cortez is a Democrat. But isn't she ANY better than Bolsonaro?

If our choice is between having one broken leg and having two broken legs plus two broken arms, is it *really* "just as bad" to vote for the one broken leg?

My Never Democrat friends have decided to cast their votes this year for a write-in candidate. They can't even get a third-party candidate they approve of officially on the ballot in one state, much less nationwide. If their "people power" only amounts to a handful of votes, maybe their candidate isn't the spoiler I fear. It seems hard, though, to justify a belief in democracy when you're admitting your vote matters so little it's "strategic" to throw it away.

Who, after all, is even going to report it on the news? What GOP or DNC leader is going to feel intimidated by such a weak showing?

"If Democrats lose two presidential elections in a row, they'll learn we mean business!"

I'm confused why they have such faith in a party they consider unredeemable.

If it's the two-party system that has already determined the ineffectiveness of voting, is a protest vote really even a protest? If the goal is to slowly, over time, educate voters, what are we persuading them to vote for if voting doesn't matter? And what happens to the hundreds of millions of oppressed people who have to wait decades for any relief?

I appreciate the demand for justice, not abandoning one segment of society to save another. I know that power never shares power unless forced to do so. But circumstances *have* changed since the election four years ago, and we must adapt or lose what little power we have to push for any change at all.

We must eliminate the Electoral College. We need ranked choice voting. We need to expand the number of viable political parties.

We need universal healthcare, tuition-free college and vocational training, government funded childcare, a Green New Deal, and much more.

We may not get any of that under Biden, but there is a possibility we could prevent outright fascist dictatorship if we elect him.

Is that not worth voting for?

If it isn't, what good is a Never Democrat's "commitment" to justice?

I'm not being snarky. It's a sincere question. If folks have ideals that simply can't be met at the current moment, what's Plan B?

I want a Democratic Socialist government. But that's not an option right now. And there is absolutely nothing about a second Trump term that advances that goal.

If our options are to eat raw chicken livers covered in horse snot OR starve to death, is one of those not a healthier choice? What if the choice is to eat raw chicken livers covered in horse snot or allow millions of *others* to starve to death?

Biden is a terrible nominee. I don't want him as president. I can think of a dozen other corporate Democrats I'd want ahead of him, and I don't want them, either. But we're no longer in a primary. I have exactly two choices in this election. One of them IS going to be president.

If we scratch our heads in confusion over why so many conservatives vote against their own self-interest, why is it OK for us to do the same ourselves?

It's possible that voting for an extremely flawed Democrat is too little too late. But can anyone honestly believe there will even be another election four years from now if we keep Trump in office? We'll have Ivanka or Don, Jr., or William Barr. Can we witness the deliberate, open dismantling of our checks and balances every day and doubt that? Trump's already encouraging chants of "Twelve more years!"

If we must cast a protest vote, can't we protest Trump instead of the DNC? *Can't we triage our protest votes?*

To be clear, I'm not going to "Unfriend" anyone who won't cast a vote for the *only* candidate that can remove Trump from office in this election. I understand this is a painful decision. Yet I'm still not going to "Re-Friend" the FB acquaintance who invests so much energy into vote shaming. Vote shaming remains negative behavior that's ineffective, even detrimental.

Yet reasoning seems ineffective, too.

So what's left? Armed insurrection? We're not white supremacists, are we?

Even if Never Democrats want a socialist revolution, when exactly are they planning to revolt? If they can't even muster enough signatures to get a candidate on the ballot, I'm not confident in their chances of succeeding at a task far more difficult.

Whether we like it or not, Biden is currently the least awful of our options. Once he and Harris are in office, once we get past whatever backlash the radical right inflicts, then we work harder than ever for the essential policies and parties we need.

In the face of the very real danger of despotism, it's ethically appropriate to do what's "pragmatic." Because anything else will allow Trump to raise our death toll even higher, with no end date in sight.

I *Want* to Give You Money, But You Must Promise to Fight for Me

I can't be the only person receiving 30 fundraising emails a day from Jon Ossoff's campaign and another 30 from Raphael Warnock's. A Democratic win of two more seats in the Senate *should* be a wonderful accomplishment after years of suffering under Republican control. But when I check the websites of both Democratic candidates for the Georgia seats, I'm baffled.

Both do have some good policy positions. No question. And both are *way* more progressive than either Loeffler or Perdue.

But neither supports Medicare for All, which poll after poll shows the majority of Americans want. They use words like "access" and "affordable." *That's not good enough*.

Both want to "reduce" the cost of higher education. They use other weasel words to avoid coming out in full support of tuition-free college and vocational training.

If they truly support these policies, but voters or donors can't find that information easily, that's still a problem. These key details certainly aren't in their emails. If the candidates support these positions, they must say so. Openly. Unequivocally. Proudly.

What I see instead is, "We need Democrats in the Senate!"

But why elect them if they won't give us the programs and policies we need? It's like planning a wedding for a marriage that will never be consummated.

So I've begun replying *to each and every email.* Here's a sample of my responses for those who might like to try a similar approach:

"Please come out publicly in support of Medicare for All."

"If you want to serve the people, and I believe you do, then you must come out in support of Medicare for All."

"Americans can't concentrate on addressing the climate crisis when they can't pay basic medical bills. Please state publicly your support for Medicare for All."

"I will donate as soon as you come out publicly in support of Medicare for All. If

you can't work for this one necessity, *what is it you think I'm gaining from your win?"*

"Your not coming out in support of Medicare for All during a pandemic that is killing more than a thousand Americans a day doesn't build confidence that you consider our existential needs a priority."

"If you want to serve the people, come out in support of Medicare for All and tuition-free college and vocational training."

"Please let me know when you come out publicly in support of Medicare for All so I can rush a donation to you in time to make a difference."

"I have limited funds and can only give to candidates who support both Medicare for All and tuition-free college and vocational training. If Democrats want to control the Senate but can't even focus on these two core principles, what exactly are they

planning to do for us? Not engage in questionable stock trades? Not be 'mean'? We need more than that."

"You must be bold to win. You must publicly support Medicare for All and give people what we need.

"Playing safe just makes you look weak both to Republicans and Democrats. Please take a bold stand and give us Medicare for All."

"Medicare for All is a MAINSTREAM position.

"I cannot donate to conservative candidates, even if they're Democrats.

"Please come out publicly in support of Medicare for All."

"A *majority* of Americans want Medicare for All. That means your position against it, by definition, is extreme. We do not need extreme, conservative Democratic senators."

"Why aren't you behind Medicare for All?

"If Democrats win the Senate in addition to the House and the White House, are you telling me you STILL won't give the people healthcare?

"Why would I sacrifice when you're telling me up front that even with full control, you can't give us the most basic of human rights?"

"I'm happy to keep receiving 30 fundraising emails from you a day, but each time you send me one, I'll remind you that I can only donate after you come out publicly in support of Medicare for All.

"Please serve your constituents by fighting for this essential program."

One of the candidates even sent out a "survey" to see what "we" wanted our elected officials to do. Here was my reply to that empty gesture:

"I answered the survey as best I could, but it's concerning that although you asked for my top three priorities, two of my top priorities weren't even on your list, which shows they're not even low priorities for you.

"No Medicare for All?

"No tuition-free college and vocational training?

"If you want to serve the American people, these items need to be at the top of your list.

"Or at least somewhere *on* your list."

"We're in the middle of a pandemic. We need Medicare for All.

"Before the pandemic, we needed Medicare for All.

"After the pandemic, we'll need Medicare for All.

"WE NEED MEDICARE FOR ALL."

"You tell us you're fighting for 'our most fundamental rights' and yet you haven't come out publicly for Medicare for All.

"I really WANT to support you, but you've GOT to be willing to fight for this most basic human right."

"Yes, I'm tired of the gridlock.

"But you're promising me up front that once the gridlock is gone, you STILL won't fight for Medicare for All.

"Or many other essential programs and policies we need.

"Removing the gridlock is only useful if *you accomplish something meaningful. And you've told me up front you won't get us the single most important thing we all need— healthcare."*

"Tired of hearing about Medicare for All?

"We're tired of *not* hearing about it."

Do my messages seem annoying? Are they frustrating to read even in this short summary? Are they obnoxious?

They certainly aren't even 1/1000 as grating as the message tens of millions of Americans hear every day— that our health, our very lives, and that of our loved ones don't really matter to the people demanding our money. The aggravation my email responses might generate is trifling compared to knowing we can't quit a hateful, dangerous job without losing our health insurance. It's nothing compared to the mental anguish underinsured Americans with no mental health coverage feel every day.

It's trivial compared with the suffering experienced by those who can't even take a sick day, with the misery Americans feel choosing between treatment for Stage 1 cancer and bankruptcy.

These two candidates *seem* to have a desperate need for my financial support. I don't expect their staff and volunteers to have time to respond to my emails. But if the candidates can't bother even to pretend to offer me the most basic of essentials *now*, when they *need* me, why should I expect them to work for me once in office?

As Elizabeth Warren once pointed out, when candidates say it's not the right time for healthcare or education or jobs, they're being completely honest that *they* will not be fighting for us if elected.

I desperately *want* to donate to Ossoff and Warnock, but they're not making it possible.

Jon? Raphael? You're running for Senate as public servants while promising not to serve. The fact that you're "better" than your opponents is of little consequence if you don't plan to address our most urgent needs.

Yes, you have *some* good policies, and we need you to stay firm on those. But we can't live on incremental progress. We can't wait thirty years to get the healthcare we need *now*. Medicare for All and tuition-free college and vocational training address basic medical, educational, and financial needs. Both are prerequisites for racial justice. These are non-negotiables.

Am I mean to pester Ossoff's and Warnock's campaigns by answering every email they send?

Well, there's a win/win solution to that.

Raphael and Jon, we want you and we need you, but only if you step up to the challenge.

It's OK to Change Our Minds

"He flip-flopped! He used to say this and now he says that! How can you trust someone who keeps changing their mind?"

We've allowed our opponents to frame changing our mind as a failure when it is in fact exactly the opposite. The only way to never change our mind is to never learn a single new fact, to never listen to a previously unheard point of view. I can't imagine anything more damning.

"Do you regret your vote to approve the war in Iraq?" we ask, hoping for a Gotcha moment. "Do you regret your support of mass incarceration?" "Do you think you were wrong to support deregulation?"

Politicians would rather go down in flames than admit they've ever made a single mistake in a thirty-year-long career. But if they can't admit it, they can't change their policy positions. Not admitting one's mistakes is perhaps the biggest mistake anyone can make, politician or not.

As a Mormon, I rallied against the Equal Rights Amendment because the "Prophet" said that women were already equal. They simply had a different role than men did. And this amendment, Latter-day Saint leaders insisted, would destroy the family. I believed my religious leaders and did as I was told.

Was that a mistake?

Of course it was! But I'm not omniscient. I can only base my decisions on the information I have at the time. As Maya Angelou said, "Do the best you can until you know better. Then when you know better, do better." It's true under virtually any circumstances.

I volunteered two years of my life to work as a Mormon missionary, telling Catholics in Rome to repent and follow the "true" church. I "bore my testimony" that the Book of Mormon was the word of God, that Joseph Smith was a prophet. In college, I gave my professors a copy of the Book of Mormon as a parting gift at the end of each semester. I paid tithing to a church that claimed homosexuality was a sin next to murder.

Do I regret my behavior as a Mormon back then?

Hell, I regret my behavior *now*! I'm still constantly making mistakes. And so is everyone else. If other people have a difficult time trusting me because I make mistakes, I'll have just as much trouble trusting them if they insist they never make errors. If I ever claim my heroes can't make mistakes, I'm doing both them and myself a disservice.

Even when I think I'm mostly right—I've been a supporter of universal healthcare for decades—the specifics of how to accomplish that goal can easily be tweaked and refined.

I've long understood we need to address the environment, conservation, and climate. But if I've been promoting wind energy and it turns out we need to focus on thermal, I can adapt to the specifics in accomplishing the overall goal.

And if the Earth is struck by a meteor or we suffer the eruption of a supervolcano and it turns out we suddenly need to battle global cooling instead, we adjust in response to the new circumstances, when we have new information.

When I was a Republican, I believed the GOP was the party of God. When I changed party affiliation and became a Democrat, I believed I'd "seen the light." Now I agree more often than not with Democratic Socialist ideas. But it's not that I disagree with *everything* Democrats or Republicans believe, even if those beliefs cause my friends to become upset with me.

I invite folks who think differently to explain their position, provide evidence, and if what they say makes sense, I'll change my mind. If not, perhaps they'll come up with some better reasoning and stronger evidence later, and I'll change my mind then. Or maybe not.

Healthcare is a human right. I'm not likely to ever change my mind about that.

But I encourage everyone to stop being afraid of being wrong. We must stop worrying about being discredited if we admit to mistakes. And we need to remember that even our greatest heroes, living or dead, can be questioned. Their words are not scripture.

And as I've learned, even "scripture" isn't necessarily the word of God.

Politics is messy. Morality is messy. Life is messy. So let's stop worrying about slipping in the mud. We *will* fall, and then we need to pull ourselves up and keep moving.

It's not just OK to change our minds. It's 100% disqualifying for a political candidate or elected official not to.

At least, that's what I believe now. Ask me again in a couple of years.

Everything to Fear Including Fear Itself

Some studies suggest that conservatives tend to focus on the negative more than liberals, have a stronger physiological reaction to perceived threats, and fear new experiences. I've heard the claims from these studies quoted by folks on the left in a kind of self-congratulatory way. *We're* better/stronger/wiser/braver than that.

But *I* feel fear all the time. My centrist Democratic friends are constantly telling me I focus too much on the negative policies pushed by their centrist heroes. And, my god, I was in my forties before I ever dared taste guacamole.

Still, I'm going to follow the example of other self-congratulatory "liberals" and point out one difference I do see between conservatives and many leftist progressives. We stand up for what's right, even when we're terrified.

When I see 18 Republican state Attorneys General backing the wild case Texas has filed with the Supreme Court to invalidate the election results of four battleground states, I'm disgusted. That disgust is magnified a thousand times when I watch 126 House Republicans add their names to an amicus brief in support of this blatant attempt to overturn an election.

Some pundits say these Republicans are "afraid" of the consequences to their own careers if they don't publicly support Trump. We see the threats and intimidation thrown against the few who do stand up. There's legitimate reason to fear.

In the past, folks like Ted Cruz, Lindsey Graham, and Marco Rubio spoke out passionately against Trump. Now they seem to worship him. Are they simply led by fear?

I'm scared every time I board a bus for work and have to sit with unmasked riders. I'm scared walking the last two blocks to the grocery, because there are no sidewalks along that stretch. I'm scared every time I give myself an insulin injection.

Every time I write a story or essay, I'm scared of making a fool of myself.

I was a virgin until I was 26, afraid because of my Mormon upbringing to accept my sexual orientation and end up condemned to Outer Darkness.

My first job after coming out was as an adjunct English instructor at a public university. Halfway through the semester, at the beginning of class, one of my students pointed to a flyer on the bulletin board. "A potluck for a gay student group? It's going to be an orgy!"

"I hate gays!" another student announced loudly. "I'll say it right to their face! I hate gays!"

I *knew* that in a class of thirty students, there had to be at least one LGBTQ student listening to this vitriol.

"Thank you," I said.

The student who'd just spoken looked pleased, but I watched as another student's head swiveled toward me and our eyes locked. She understood immediately.

"I'm gay," I continued.

The student who'd proudly declared his hatred started spluttering. "Oh! Well, you're still a good teacher! You're still a good teacher!"

I laughed, knowing that my abilities as a teacher, or lack thereof, were completely unrelated to my orientation. But I did at the very least take advantage of that day's "teaching moment."

I have been "out" in every job I've worked since then. That doesn't mean "flaunting" my sexuality. It means using the correct pronouns. It means not lying.

A friend of mine was stabbed to death by a gay basher. I understand there are real consequences to being out. But even if I were to discover at Judgment Day that the Mormons were right and I was going to spend the rest of my existence in Outer Darkness, I see no reason to start living in Hell right now.

And being too afraid to stand up for my rights, the rights of others, for democracy, to stand up against bullying and tyranny and corruption, would be to embrace a hellish existence today.

I see my old right-wing missionary pals on Facebook ridiculing mask wearers for "letting fear rule their lives."

I admit, I'm afraid. When I see a police car parked across the street from my house for no apparent reason, I'm nervous. When I take part in a Black Lives Matter protest, I'm scared. When my husband volunteers as security at a counterprotest against the Proud Boys, I'm worried.

Once, when I was eleven (God, I hope I wasn't any older than that!) I peed on the carpet in my bedroom and blamed it the next day on my chihuahua because to reach the bathroom, I'd have had to make it all the way down a long hallway, in the dark, after midnight.

Do you believe me now when I tell you that by nature I'm a scaredy-cat?

I worry that my political essays will impact my ability to get a job interview in the future. I worry about a prospective employer looking me up online and finding my views on polyamory. As someone who used to worship alongside a Holocaust survivor, I experience every day what to me is real fear that I'm going to hear a knock on my door and be taken away.

I used to marvel at how Christian women protested on Rosenstrasse to liberate their Jewish husbands. I marveled at Chinese pro-democracy students standing up against military tanks. I stared in admiration as a Black woman stood her ground while riot police descended upon her.

I understand, though, that every one of these folks was probably terrified. They simply did what had to be done regardless.

When I watch so many elected Republican officials publicly support Trump because they're afraid not to, I'm scared as well. I also feel pity for their weak character. And anger that these brave "patriots" can't do the bare minimum on behalf of democracy.

Life doesn't always turn out well for those who do the right thing despite their fear. But it often doesn't work out very well for collaborators, either.

I'm scared. I expect you're scared, too. We'd be fools not to be. We *know* what happens when dictators take over. But I want to alleviate at least *one* of your fears.

Being afraid *doesn't* mean you're a closeted, right-wing conservative at heart.

The Cult of Trump Is the New Westboro Baptist Church

Orange is the New Black. Man buns are the new mullet.

And the Cult of Trump is the new Westboro Baptist Church.

When I hear Trump supporters jeering Biden as he pays respects to his dead wife and daughter, when I see them giddily burning Black Lives Matter banners, when I see folks with MAGA hats rallying in the rain waving signs that proclaim the virus is a hoax, I realize Trump devotees haven't just turned worship of the man into a cult, they've turned it into one barely distinguishable from the hateful antics and rhetoric of the Westboro Baptist Church.

Though I've only just come to this realization, it should have been obvious the moment Trump mocked a disabled reporter on live TV and his followers considered him the new winner of Last Comic Standing.

They're like Westboro members waving signs that say "God Hates Fags" or "Thank God for Dead Soldiers" or "God Sent the Shooters" and "Thank God for 9/11."

Westboro members so firmly believe in their message of hate that they even carry signs declaring "God Is Your Enemy."

But Westboro is mostly a tiny, fringe cult with little real power. If we step that up to the next level, we get a Jonestown cult.

Jackie Speier, the California congresswoman who survived an attack by Jim Jones supporters, said that when she was first asked if this cult of Donald Trump seemed to her anything like that of Jim Jones, she was horrified at the suggestion. But as she watched the cult develop, she concluded that the two cults are, in fact, quite similar.

Comparisons to either cult are disturbing, but we all know that the danger posed by this cult is several orders of magnitude greater, mostly because society as a whole saw Fred Phelps and Jim Jones as fringe crackpots while the cult of Trump has become thoroughly normalized. It would be a difference along the lines of the Manson Family vs. the Cossacks.

As a devout Mormon, I belonged to a global community that normalized several cult-like behaviors, whether it was chanting in the temple while wearing green aprons and bakers' hats or devoting two years of my life as a missionary sworn to avoid watching television or reading newspapers or ever being without my assigned "companion."

In one meeting in Rome, every missionary was required to bear his or her "testimony." If someone refused, we were all forced to wait...and wait...and wait...until the rebellious missionary gave in.

"I know the Church is true." It showed a lack of faith to say "believe."

After returning to America, I remained deeply involved in my religious community. As a Mormon in New Orleans, I was part of an extremely small group, and yet Mormonism was my entire life.

And when I dared to declare openly that I was gay, I was excommunicated and shunned. Friends I'd known for years refused to speak to me, would cross the chapel to avoid shaking my hand.

They deemed their behavior normal, even praiseworthy, as they congratulated each other on keeping themselves pure by avoiding contact with me.

The Church of Jesus Christ of Latter-day Saints was a mainstream religion and yet still operated in many ways as a cult. I'd been highly regarded one day, a leader in the Elders Quorum and the Single Adult group, and the next day, I was an apostate. Just as a Republican hero like Governor Kemp of Georgia can be called a traitor because he wouldn't manipulate the election results to favor Trump.

Once anyone, Mormon or not, speaks out against a Mormon teaching, he or she is instantly labeled an anti-Mormon. Anything they say, no matter how grounded in fact, instantly becomes a lie. It's normal in that community.

As it is now for almost half the country taking part in a cult just as cruel and detached from reality. Trump is the only source of absolute truth. He is the Prophet.

When I was a Mormon, I laughed when people told me I belonged to a cult.

But I learned that the difference between a cult and a religion is normalization. And it's the same difference when we're talking about politics.

The Cult of Trump is destroying the Republican Party. And it's destroying America.

The solution isn't to become more desperately delusional.

When I belonged to a cult, I said and did and believed obnoxious things. But I finally broke free. America can do the same.

And when Trump supporters start making the effort to accept reality, let's help by refusing to treat them the way they treated us *and* each other.

Punishing Sedition *Won't* Only Divide Us Further

We hear it over and over. "Impeaching Trump/charging insurrectionists/holding GOP leaders accountable for lying about the election will only further divide us."

As infuriating as those words are, the fact is they're true. What's also true is that *no* course of action exists that will please Trump supporters/party over country supporters/collaborators.

Well, no course other than complete surrender and abdication of our rights.

We see the dynamic repeatedly. A burglar breaks into a house, is surprised by a homeowner brandishing a gun, and shoots the homeowner in "self-defense." Or perhaps it's not a burglar breaking in but a police officer with a no-knock warrant. Or a patriot threatening Black Lives Matter protesters. "I feared for my life," the accused killer says. "I wasn't there to hurt anyone."

In a scene from the classic film *Bonnie and Clyde*, the infamous outlaws rob a bank and jump into their getaway car. But a determined bank employee chases after them, jumping onto the vehicle's running board. Clyde doesn't *want* to shoot him, but he's *forced* to. If only the stupid, petty guard would have let him steal all that money without making such a fuss.

This was Bonnie and Clyde's first murder, but as the movie (and the real-life events it portrayed) develop, the outlaws kill again. And again.

And killing others gets easier each time.

Accountability is non-negotiable, but accountability doesn't mean revenge. After WWI, allies "punished" Germany so severely that they created conditions making it easier for the German people to follow a murderous dictator who would "save" them.

After WWII, however, while the U.S. held both Germany and Japan accountable, it also helped them with the Marshall Plan and other aid programs. The aid came with many conditions, of course, some of which were paradoxically harmful. But both former enemies became allies as a result of accountability combined with cooperation.

Accountability *can* bring both peace and unity if enacted appropriately.

Letting bullies, criminals, tyrants, and corruption go unaddressed, on the other hand, can never bring the peace and unity Republican apologists are pretending to believe it will.

If GOP lawmakers and right-wing pundits truly desire to bring people together, they can start by disavowing the lie that the election was stolen from Trump. Truth offers a path to healing. Lies and excuses never will.

Apologizing for their bad behavior will go a long way toward rebuilding trust and integrity, too.

Complaints over being called out for supporting an insurrection, however, do nothing to make America great again.

Punishing sedition *will* divide us further. That is unfortunately true. But it won't "only" divide us. It will also offer accountability and a chance to carve out a safer, healthier path forward.

We Can't Let Sunk Costs Sink Us

We've all made irrational decisions because of sunk costs. Perhaps we're three years into a degree before realizing we want to pursue an entirely different career. Maybe we've invested $50,000 into a renovation before discovering it would have been better to sell and move to a new home.

Or maybe we've supported a political party or a specific candidate so long and faced so much opposition for it that we can't admit we were wrong.

We mustn't let sunk costs sink us.

Those of us wondering how our friends and family can be QAnon followers or still believe the pandemic is a hoax need to understand the psychological trauma someone must willingly accept to change their mind about something so monumental.

So let's try to feel some empathy.

Perhaps we put twelve years into a marriage we realized was doomed after six, because we'd worked so hard already, had a child, had developed relationships with our spouse's friends and family. Maybe if we work a bit harder, we think, hang on a little longer, things will still work out.

And then, after years of additional grief, we finally face reality and file for divorce. The delay, of course, has only made things worse. Now we have *two* children who will be affected. Now we're risking even deeper relationships with friends and family. And we're older, less "marketable" to find love elsewhere, more damaged emotionally from the additional years of unhappiness.

We're *embarrassed* we allowed ourselves to be miserable for so long. We feel *stupid.*

Many white Americans have invested so much into believing a glorified history of the United States that we simply can't face listening to the reality of racial abuse. We're worried that doing so makes us responsible for things others have done. We're leery it will make us responsible to change our own behavior.

We are, quite simply, afraid.

So we let that sunk cost keep us from making life better not only for others but for ourselves as well.

Perhaps we've spent years as a three-car family, flown across the country, even to Europe or Asia, on vacation. We've invested both financially and emotionally into believing the climate crisis isn't real. Accepting the truth now means not only that we must make drastic adjustments to our lifestyles but also that we accept our role in making the problem worse because we *chose* not to believe the evidence.

That's a blow almost no ego can sustain.

In the movie *Awakenings*, the true story of a physician who awakens survivors of a sleeping sickness epidemic, we see patients who became ill in their youth finally returning to life in their fifties and sixties. At first, they're out dancing and enjoying life again. Everything looks great. What a success story.

Then a hospital staff member cheerfully asks someone how they feel about this miracle.

"I feel cheated," the man says angrily. He'd fallen asleep at seventeen and now he's an old man.

Jehovah's Witnesses and Hasidic Jews and Mormons and others sometimes decide late in life that the religion they've dedicated their lives to isn't "true." On reddit recently, a woman recounted the dismay she felt upon realizing she'd paid half a million dollars in tithing over a lifetime to an organization she no longer believed in. She was sixty-five, finally retired, but instead of freedom felt only the loss of "the best years of her life."

If we've spent our lives as Republicans, or Democrats, or as apolitical non-voters, but now think we made a mistake, if we spent the last five years supporting someone we believed wholeheartedly and now realize was lying, if we've lost friends and family because we believed conspiracy theories, then, consciously or not, we're likely afraid of facing the truth. Who wouldn't be?

We know it means admitting we were wrong, admitting we were, on some level, the "bad guy." Or, at best, a fool, which isn't much easier to face.

We *all* make bad decisions at some point in our lives.

But we have a choice. We can continue to waste more time, more money, more life…or we can try to salvage what's left.

As Maya Angelou said, "Do the best you can until you know better. Then when you know better, do better."

We must not let sunk costs sink us.

Want to Heal and Unify America?
Then Enact Bold Change

"We must heal and unify our divided nation. We must look forward, not back."

We can't look forward, of course, until we address past behavior, and that means accountability for those who have done the most to tear this nation apart.

But aside from that, the main reason folks everywhere along the political spectrum are hurting and divided to begin with is because their most basic needs are not being met, not only during the pandemic or these past four years, but for many decades.

"We don't want to be radical like the right has been. We see how dangerous radical policies are."

Poll after poll shows that the majority of Americans support universal healthcare. That's not radical.

We cannot heal and unify our nation without enacting BOLD change.

Do "liberals" and "progressives" want a life without debt? Why, yes, we do.

But "conservatives" and "independents" aren't crazy about a lifetime of debt, either. Not for themselves, anyway.

Both the incoming administration and Congress must understand that tuition-free college and vocational training help *all* voters. Well, at least 99% of them. But if those in Washington, or in state legislatures, are worried about that top 1%, perhaps you're not truly concerned about healing and unifying the American people.

We cannot move forward as a nation unless we address our voting crisis. Every adult must be registered automatically. If we want to require special ID, that ID must also be provided by the government. We must eliminate gerrymandering from both the right and left. We must abolish the Electoral College. Paper ballots that provide a paper trail are absolutely essential.

"Radical policies will divide us."

If your policy is to abolish the minimum wage or ban unions, then yes, you'd be right. But if your policies work to improve the lives of the working class *and* middle class, if your policies provide healthcare for all who need it, ensure an educated, skilled workforce, guarantee that all votes are counted equally and every election result easily verified, you will bring healing and unification.

We can be sure, of course, the top 1% won't like us. Perhaps not even the top 5%. But we'll have the support of everyone else.

Many on the right have been brainwashed—sorry, there's no better term—to believe that twenty years of student loan debt is a plus. They've been brainwashed not to believe the science proving climate change. A good many Democrats have been brainwashed as well, to believe that it's more important not to go against Republican talking points than it is to make life better for voters.

So we'll need to work with cult deprogrammers—I'm not being sarcastic—and use emotional appeals in addition to logic.

But if Democrats are not up to the challenge, why do you think we'd ever vote for you or your party again?

Those on the right will protest when you make bold policy changes. But unless you really haven't been paying attention, you know they'll protest even when you make tiny ones. Accept that and make the changes we need, the changes we voted you in to make.

The new administration can only be sure of its power in the White House, Senate, and House of Representatives for the next two years. And if you don't act boldly right from the start, you'll never accomplish anything at all.

You'll have failed voters on all sides. Democrats will lose faith and Republicans won't be won over. You'll lose majorities in the 2022 elections, and you'll embolden a stronger and more dangerous "conservative" to replace the one we just voted out.

We *all* need bold action on the climate crisis. But if you do no more than ban fracking and coal mining, you'll only have addressed a small part of the problem. You must retrain and find other jobs for displaced workers.

If you want compliance when you close small businesses because of the pandemic, you must pay people to stay home and stay closed.

If all you can bring is misery each time you make an "improvement," you can't possibly win over voters.

If you want to heal and unify, and we all hope you do, you must address the basic needs of the American people.

Mormon Communists with
Temple Recommends

Many Mormons in Utah see Mitt Romney as a traitor, a lefty radical, because he won't support Trump's most egregious acts of oppression. Mormons need to start separating their religious convictions from the Republican party line.

"Valeria" was one my favorite missionaries when I served in the Italy Rome Mission. She was also a Communist. Her older sister had been baptized in southern Italy when Valeria was 16, too young to be baptized herself without parental approval. Their uncle was a Catholic priest who lived and worked in a church on the ground floor of the family home in Puglia. Valeria only spoke in glowing terms about the man, unhappy when LDS missionaries made derogatory comments about Catholic clergymen. But she continued to study Mormonism secretly, and when she turned 18, she cut her hair short to celebrate her transition to adulthood.

At least that's what she told her parents. Valeria really cut her hair so it would dry quickly after she was secretly baptized. Months passed before her mother discovered a Book of Mormon hidden under her mattress, resulting in a beating so severe that Valeria's father had to physically tear his wife away before their daughter was seriously injured.

Valeria was "grounded" for the next couple of years, only allowed out of the house on brief, monitored errands and visits. But she was plotting something else. She submitted her mission papers and was called to serve as a missionary in Rome. The Church would pay her expenses.

Valeria broke the news to her parents the day before she caught the train north.

One of my early companions, in Ciampino, was the first to tell me about this extraordinary woman. I didn't meet Valeria myself until I'd been transferred to Napoli 2, the first district I'd served which had a contingent of sister missionaries. They were all fairly impressive, one time sending the most agile member of their group out a stairwell window to crawl along a ledge to break into our apartment the day we reneged on a promise of providing Fast Sunday dinner.

One morning during district meeting, Valeria told us that the previous evening, she and her companion were about to enter the next building in their tracting zone when they suddenly felt "the Spirit" warn them not to go in. They moved on to the next building and began knocking on doors. It was there they learned the apartments they'd skipped had been condemned after an earthquake several months earlier.

I worked with Valeria again in Rome 4, even tracting along with her and her new companion. That companion was a bit overbearing and critical, but Valeria never complained. I often spoke in Italian with her after district meetings because the other missionaries talked to each other in English, leaving her out of conversations. Valeria confided that she'd slowly been rebuilding a relationship with her mother and felt secure enough to mail home the Church books she'd accumulated during her mission. They were just too heavy to keep carrying in her suitcase every time she was transferred.

Her mother threw the books away.

Valeria never stooped to blurting out even the softest of expletives. No "caspita" or "mannaggia" or anything else that would have been as gentle as "darn" or "flip" among the English-speaking missionaries. She rarely judged others, though she did mention once she disapproved of my Italian companion using the word "cacca."

Valeria and I became pen pals after we completed our missions, sending physical letters in the days before email. A year later, I returned to Florence for a summer language course. She caught the train to stay with a friend in nearby Siena. We dated every day for two weeks, strolling past the Duomo, holding hands crossing the Ponte Vecchio, attending church meetings with the local Mormons.

I caught a train south with her, the cheapest tickets allowing us only a couple of feet on the floor in front of the bathroom for the 13-hour trip. I stayed at the home of one of Valeria's friends and, after another two weeks of dating, I proposed. Mormons, after all, are notorious for quick engagements, and I knew I'd never meet a better woman. It was only after she accepted my proposal that Valeria made her first and only demand—pasta would only be served al dente.

We planned to live with her parents, but I wanted to finish my degree first, so I returned to America. A year later, she came to visit me in New Orleans for a month. And we continued a long-distance engagement for another two years after that. It wasn't only the unfinished degree holding me back from bringing Valeria to the temple, though. I was also committed to becoming straight before we took that next step.

We wrote long letters on Sundays and scribbled postcards on Wednesdays. A couple of times a year, we spoke on the phone, crazy expensive at the time. And for Valeria's birthday, I always sent a box full of Jell-O, peanut butter cups, cheesecake mix, and peanut butter, items she'd grown to love which were unavailable in her town. I even threw in a Snickers and a Butterfinger, and Valeria would ration out the goodies over the next several months.

One day, I made an unscheduled phone call, paying attention to the time difference to give her the unpleasant news early enough that she'd still have an opportunity to seek out the support of others. "Sono omosessuale," I said, "un finocchio."

Taken aback, she told me, "Well, you take care of that and then we'll get married."

Instead, I was excommunicated for being gay, and almost every friend I'd ever had at church cut me out of their lives.

Valeria didn't. We continued writing, I continued sending her birthday packages, and we remained friends until her death from breast cancer in her mid-fifties.

She'd taken care of both her parents in their final years. She remained an active, stalwart member of her congregation, teaching Sunday School, giving talks, and making the long trip up to Switzerland regularly to attend the nearest Mormon temple, the temple where she did finally marry another temple-worthy returned missionary like herself a few years before she died.

After receiving her first temple recommend to serve as a missionary, Valeria passed every annual recommend interview for the rest of her life.

She was a registered Communist most of that time.

In an odd twist of fate, the man I eventually married turned out to be one of the elders who first taught Valeria and her sister all those years earlier. He was also, of course, excommunicated for being gay.

And he's a socialist, something Mormons in America deem equivalent to Devil worship. It's not something Mormons elsewhere worry much about. Members of the Church in the U.S. would do well to separate their religious beliefs from their political party platform. One can be quite far to the left and still be a good Mormon. And a good person.

After Valeria accepted my proposal, she offered me the opportunity to read her journal. The following morning, I teased her, pointing out her words, "He's not the man of my dreams, but..."

She looked mortified and then smiled. "I'll just have to make sure to dream about you tonight!"

Valeria was a sweet, kind woman, a dedicated missionary, a devout Mormon, a temple recommend holder. The only woman I've ever kissed. And a Communist.

Mormon leaders have asked us to "Give Joseph Smith a break!" and stop demanding a history of perfection. It would be a good idea for Mormons to give Mitt Romney a break, too, and stop demanding he give up his principles to support Republican leaders at all costs.

Mormons should give themselves a break, too, and do the same thing.

Culture also means that back when "the majority"
~~d~~ LGBTQ folks were unacceptable, it was OK to
~~~~ actors. It means that back when "the majority" felt
~~~~g a communist meeting even once meant you were
~~~~ting treason, destroying careers and creating a
~~~~ood blacklist were justified.

~~~~ill not purposely watch another movie starring Tom
~~~~, but that doesn't mean I won't re-watch *Coma* or
Out just because he's in them. And it doesn't mean
~~~~he should be banned from all future acting jobs.

~~~~ncel Culture in terms of our personal relationships
~~~~problematic. I was still a Republican when I became
~~~~d to a woman who belonged to the Communist
~~~~ Italy. I didn't try to change her views and she
~~~~ry to change mine. Over time, I became a Democrat
~~~~n a progressive Democrat and then a Democratic
~~~~st. My husband, though, is a Trotsky socialist.
~~~~ he divorce me because I haven't moved as far to
~~~~ as he has? It took me a while, after all, even to
~~~~I was gay.

~~~~me of my moderate Democrat friends support
~~~~ates who endorse fracking, further contributing to a
~~~~ crisis displacing millions and accelerating a
~~~~vide disaster. So do I dump all my moderate
~~~~rat friends?

~~~~on't sweat the small stuff."

~~~~nying healthcare to thirty million Americans isn't
~~~~ficant. Eliminating EPA guidelines isn't a minor

Do Lose Friends over Politics

"Pick your battles."

"Don't sweat the small stuff."

"Don't lose friends over politics."

When Ellen DeGeneres was called out for joking and laughing with former president George W. Bush as they watched a football game together, she defended her friendship with the man who pushed us into an unjustified war against Iraq. "When I say, 'Be kind to one another,' I don't mean only the people who think the same way that you do. I mean be kind to everyone. Doesn't matter."

So would Ellen "be kind" to someone who considers LGBTQ people dangerous criminals who shouldn't be allowed in the classroom? Would she "be kind" to someone who claims blacks are inferior and should be disenfranchised whenever possible? Would she "be kind" to someone who argues that women should know their place and not receive equal pay?

I remember Lily Tomlin walking off the set when Chad Everett made sexist comments. That sounds far more appropriate to me.

"Everyone" includes a great many people with beliefs and political agendas that are completely unacceptable. It's disingenuous to pretend otherwise.

When my Mormon family members say they love me but then continue paying over $10,000 a year in tithes supporting a religion which in turn spends millions to oppress LGBTQ folks via secular laws, I don't feel particularly loved. Is it "quibbling" to point out the LDS Church still opposes the Equal Rights Amendment? Everyone gives others a pass once in a while, but do we keep giving them a pass for fifty years?

I dated a former Catholic priest who told me that women who were raped usually brought it on themselves by the clothes they wore. I could have tried to educate him, but I made another choice. I broke up with him.

A friend of mine once said she supported gay rights but thought the idea of gay marriage was ridiculous. "Marriage is for having kids," she said.

I genuinely liked this friend and decided our friendship was worth a bit of effort. "So you think a middle-aged widow and widower shouldn't be allowed to marry? That a marriage should be annulled if one spouse is determined to be infertile or sterile? That couples should be refused a marriage license until they're ready to have kids, that if they don't reproduce within the first year or two, they've broken their contract with the state and their marriage should be dissolved?"

My friend backed down. Of coɩ knowing if she had really changed didn't feel the need to break into he her diary, either. As long as she particular anti-LGBTQ argument to with whatever slow pace she migh understanding. If, however, she had ɩ just donated $200 to support a candid a homophobic agenda, we'd have ha and I would have reevaluated our fr end of that exchange.

"I feel like I'm always walking o friend told me.

"You are," I replied. "And so aɩ times, need to make sure we're not don't need to be nasty when calling eɑ that's almost certainly counterprodu counterproductive, too.

Cancel Culture is a double-edged for the end of someone's career becaɩ made, either today or fifteen years in t room for growth, for apologies, for ɩ moving forward. Some actions or unforgiveable, but few of us are comɩ age of 18. I have certainly said insensitive, and damaging things ove fewer inappropriate comments now buɩ never make another mistake. I'd l continue progressing rather than be

Cancel believe fire ga attendi commi Hollyw

I v Sellecɩ *In and* I think

Cɑ is also engage Party didn't and th Sociaɩ Shoulɩ the leɩ accepɩ

Sɩ candic globaɩ planeɩ Demoɩ

"ɩ

D insigɩ

difference of opinion. Anti-trans legislation isn't something to be shrugged off. Supporting an agency that separates migrant children from their parents isn't trivial.

"Don't lose friends over politics."

Only someone with privilege, someone who will do just fine no matter which candidate wins, could ever say such a thing.

We don't want to live in an echo chamber and we certainly don't want our loved ones to. Yet if a friend or family member doesn't "actively" hurt us or others but does actively support candidates who do, the transitive property comes into play.

"Pick your battles."

I do. And one of those battles is with the gaslighting that differences of "opinion" don't matter. Sometimes, they're a matter of life or death for the people you claim to love.

Joan Crawford as American History

Watching the FX series *Feud* about the rivalry between Bette Davis and Joan Crawford, I was struck by the power and resilience Joan displayed, overcoming childhood neglect and sexual abuse to get her start in the film industry in several "stag" movies before continuing on to Hollywood stardom and winning an Oscar. At a time when women were has-beens in the industry by the age of 35, she found ways to keep acting well past her "prime." She was truly a formidable, impressive woman who beat the odds again and again through sheer will. A rags-to-riches American success story.

And she was, by all accounts, a despicable human being. *Mommie Dearest* barely scratches the surface. Joan Crawford was demonstrably cruel, manipulative, and just plain mean.

Is it wrong for me then to enjoy the cult classic, *What Ever Happened to Baby Jane?* Should I allow myself to watch *Mildred Pierce* or *The Women* or *Humoresque*? How about two other films for which she received Academy Award nominations? The episode of *Night Gallery* directed by Steven Spielberg? Or any of her other 90+ credits? Can I truly appreciate American cultural history, the history of American cinema, without watching at least a few Joan Crawford movies?

I sometimes wonder if too many of us are overly self-reflective, if we analyze everything to death, but Joan Crawford's terrible character flaws do raise questions. Is it possible to enjoy the good in a person or institution while acknowledging the bad? Do I have to *like* Joan Crawford to appreciate her contribution? Do I not watch *any* movies produced by the abusive Hollywood studio system of the Golden Age?

And the abuse didn't stop there. We wonder if we can still enjoy *Shakespeare in Love*, even if Harvey Weinstein was the producer. Is it possible to respect the artistry in Amy Winehouse's "Rehab," even knowing she died later of an overdose? Must we never watch *Amadeus* or *Ferris Bueller's Day Off* because of Jeffrey Jones?

Frankly—no pun intended—I can't bear to watch any Sinatra movie after learning what a creep and diva he was. But my revulsion doesn't change the beauty or power of his voice. The 1990 version of *Hamlet* is still one of my favorite adaptations, even if I'd rather Mel Gibson wasn't earning residuals.

Conservatives, who both complain about and insist on enforcing a Cancel Culture, are afraid that "America" will be cancelled if we admit there are not only mistakes in our past but horrendous atrocities even in the present day. But protesters and activists are not trying to cancel America. We're asking it to live up to its ideals. Ideals that conservatives and religious evangelicals support. We're asking Americans to take responsibility for our actions and pull ourselves up by our bootstraps.

I can be grateful George Washington helped free (white) America from England while still acknowledging he owned slaves from the time he was eleven, that he continued to own other human beings till the day he died, and refused even to allow their release until his wife succeeded him in death. Slavery is OK, I suppose, if it proves you love your wife. Conservatives would have us believe the *only* way we can appreciate Washington's contribution to our lives is to delude ourselves that he *didn't* inflect irreparable harm on the lives of others.

But we are perfectly capable of acknowledging both truths at the same time.

I like chocolate but I don't like chocolate ice cream. Confusing? Impossible! The beginning of the apocalypse?

No. Just a simple fact.

It's possible to acknowledge police departments provide a useful service to the community while simultaneously declaring that some of their actions are unacceptable and must be stopped. I can be grateful for the service of our military men and women overseas without giving anyone a pass on "enhanced interrogation."

Really. I can do that. I don't even find it difficult.

I can appreciate Martin Luther King's great qualities without any need to deny his extramarital relationships. I can recognize how fortunate I was to spend two years in Italy as a Mormon missionary while admitting the cultural imperialism I practiced was shameful.

I'm baffled that so many of us feel compelled to view everything in either/or terms. *Either* the Constitution was a powerful step forward in our cultural history *or* it's completely worthless because it didn't ban slavery. The Constitution, its amendments, and the Bill of Rights are important documents that did help push human rights forward *and* they're terribly flawed, hindering the realization of equality for non-white people even today.

My mother loved me and made my life (mostly) wonderful. *And* she was blatantly racist and classist. I can't think of a single person in my life who wasn't a mixture of both good and bad, including me. Why in the world would we expect any author, actor, or human rights advocate to be perfect? Why expect any document they produced to be perfect? Is it even possible to achieve such perfection?

My imperfect father was still within his rights to punish me when I talked back to him. I was well within my rights to fail a student's research paper when I discovered it was plagiarized. Accepting reality doesn't keep us from punishing bad behavior and rewarding good behavior. We can implement ways to improve both our assessment and achievement of what is acceptable. We can raise our goals, demand more of ourselves and others, improve and progress and help others do the same.

I made a D the first time I took Algebra in 8th grade. I made an A when I took it again in 9th grade and was chosen to represent my school in a citywide scholastic exam. Performing poorly doesn't mean we can't do better. Doing well doesn't mean we started out perfect. This does not need to be a difficult, politicized concept. Reality doesn't need to be partisan.

But we can't improve if we believe our heroes and institutions are faultless. If "the Church" is perfect, if America is by definition unreproachable, we'd have to believe we're living in Paradise right now, and it's clear—I hope—we aren't. Things *aren't* perfect, and they *can* be improved, so for God's sake, let's go ahead and improve them.

Why is that so threatening?

Joan Crawford never achieved any kind of redemption as far as I can tell. She seems to have existed in a permanent state of denial, refusing any responsibility for her problems. They were everyone else's fault.

Likewise, there are parts of our criminal justice system and other aspects of our culture that probably can't be salvaged. We'll need to hire a different actress if we don't want to go crazy filming the next masterpiece. The choice, we need to remember, isn't just between Bette and Joan. There's a whole host of other actors to choose from.

If denying reality is the only way we can face the future, that can only mean our present perception is based on lies. That's not sustainable. Shouting our lies ever more loudly, beating and imprisoning anyone telling the truth, won't *change* reality in any way. Pretending you don't have appendicitis won't prevent you from dying of sepsis.

To be clear, this isn't simply a condemnation of anti-science Republicans but is just as true for Democrats who accept whatever party leaders tell them, never demanding accountability and progress on the issues that matter. I've been hearing promises of "later" and "next time" for decades. At some point, we must accept we're denying reality ourselves.

As a former devout Mormon, I can testify that accepting the evidence that my entire worldview was based on lies was painful, infuriating, and confusing. But I did accept reality and moved on. Life after this kind of paradigm shift may not be Paradise, either, but basing my decisions and behavior on facts has been far more rewarding than anything that preceded it. And as I learn new facts, I adjust again as necessary. I feel no obligation to remain stuck in a second worldview. Or a third. Adjusting is almost always scary but remaining trapped and stagnant is far more frightening.

America's future can be greater than any lie we've ever believed about it. It's never going to be possible to make America great "again," but we *can* make America great. Let's accept reality so we can work together to achieve it.

The God Lottery

As a Mormon attending a Baptist high school, I often wondered how I ended up so lucky. How could I have won the religion lottery and be part of an extremely tiny fraction of humans who had ever heard of The Church of Jesus Christ of Latter-day Saints? Our prophet and apostles told us it was because we'd been extra valiant in the Pre-Existence, but that struck me as an awfully convenient response.

The question became more pressing when I was "called" to serve as a missionary in Italy. How did a kid from the suburbs of New Orleans end up with privileged information that Catholics in Rome hadn't been worthy to receive without me?

If both Anne Frank *and* Adolph Hitler could have "their work" done for them in the temple so they'd have a chance at accepting "the truth" in the afterlife, what did it matter which religion, if any at all, we followed here in the first place?

I continued questioning, continued learning, and within a few years had left my church. After a few years as a Reform Jew, I could eventually no longer even remain part of that far more progressive group. I still maintained a general belief in God and an afterlife but accepted that there was no way to have any clear idea of what either might be like.

So *did* it matter? Even if it did, there was nothing I could do about it.

When the existence of God began posing more of a threat than a comfort, I wondered if I should even *want* to believe. If there *was* a God, I was going to use my best Ricky Ricardo impression when we finally met. "You've got some 'splainin' to do!"

In the years since, I've found no intellectually persuasive argument to support a belief in "God." Even as a believer, I found Rabbi Harold Kushner's book, *Who Needs God?* unconvincing. I continued to believe, though, because I *wanted* people to be genuinely happy one day, and believing seemed the only way to hang onto that hope. Eventually, the dishonesty became unbearable, and I had to admit to myself that my "belief" was as pathetic as Florence Foster Jenkins's delusion regarding her singing talent.

The thing is, I don't want "God" merely because I want emotional peace or an end to suffering, as great as both might be. What I want is for all we go through *to matter*. I want it to matter that I tried so hard, even if I failed. I want it to matter that other people accomplish great and humane things. I hear atheist friends tell me, "You find your own reasons to give meaning to life." But I can't just *pretend* it matters simply because I've invented a "reason."

Wouldn't that just be lying to myself? I didn't enjoy living a lie when I was trying to be heterosexual. And inner integrity is far more essential to my core than my affectional orientation.

Fortunately, or unfortunately, as the case may be, I've finally been able to create a personal philosophy that allows me to believe. It is clearly as ridiculous as any I've heard elsewhere, but for now, it works for me. Like millions of other fools, I regularly play the lottery, even knowing the odds are astronomically stacked against me. I could spend a million dollars on a single drawing and still have only a 1 in 200 chance of winning. Not great odds for such an investment.

But people *do* win the lottery every few weeks. It happens. It's "possible." I make a deliberate choice every week to believe it could be me. *Someone* who's made the same embarrassing choice *will* win.

So while I don't currently have even one convincing reason to believe in a just God, I can also accept that it's *remotely* possible an acceptable reason *exists* for God to allow widespread, near constant misery for billions of people. Otherwise, it's God's existence that doesn't matter, not our lives. If he/she/it treats us like crap here, why would we expect different treatment in "heaven"? Six decades of my life is a far greater investment than the million dollars I might have been willing to invest in state lottery tickets.

I've decided on a God Lottery as justification for choosing to believe. The chances that a Supreme Being exists and there is some version of a "life after death" are astronomically slim, but it's *possible*, however unlikely. I can't make plans dependent on possible lottery winnings, no matter how many times I buy a ticket on a trip to the grocery. I still need to go to work and earn money and fight for universal healthcare and fair elections and all the rest *as if* I'll never win because it's almost certain I won't. But I don't give up purchasing a ticket week after week simply because finances may be tough right now. I can sing Wilson Phillips's, "Hold On," knowing I *might* have more money in a few weeks. It's a delusion that can potentially be as harmful as helpful. If we believe things will be better "later," perhaps we won't fight as hard to make them better *now*.

But I still don't think it's as bad a philosophy as Pascal's Wager, which only posits two choices. Either there's no god or there is a god, and since our eternal happiness rests on the answer, it's best to act as if there is one. Many have pointed out, of course, that this wager assumes there is only one possible god. How would the wager look if the choice were between no god, the Abrahamic god, any of the Greek gods, Norse gods, Hindu gods, indigenous gods, and so forth? Instead of having a 50/50 chance of being right, we now have a 1 in 500 chance, a far more problematic wager.

My "belief" may be no more than a "white lie" I tell myself rather than an outright falsehood. But I expect my views on the subject will continue to evolve, hopefully in an ever healthier direction.

Still, I don't think creating the fiction of a God Lottery makes me agnostic. I'm an atheist believer. It's not the same thing.

And you thought the Trinity was a difficult concept.

I can be as poor a theologian as anyone. And so can you.

So I pray that we can all choose to believe in principles that both give meaning to our lives and help us make life better for others at the same time.

And I say this in the name of...oh, hell.

Just for the Outer Darkness of It

"Greater love hath no man than this, that a man lay down his life for a friend" (John 15:13).

A few years back, a television commercial featured a young girl watching her mother rinse the dishes before placing them in the dishwasher. "I thought the dishwasher did the dishes," the young girl says, puzzled.

"It does," the mother replies with a big smile, washing another plate before setting it in the dishwasher.

The young girl looks on in confusion.

Mormon theology explaining why we face Earthly trials is every bit as confusing.

We are deeply moved when we see stories of people sacrificing their freedom or their life for others, Corrie ten Boom hiding Jews and ultimately being sent to a concentration camp along with them, Aleksandr Solzhenitsyn sentenced to eight years of hard labor in a gulag for opposing Stalin, firefighters dying in the World Trade Center as they tried to rescue office workers. When soldiers die in battle, we commemorate them for making the ultimate sacrifice.

Mormons seem to follow this same basic line of reasoning. We think of those killed at Haun's Mill as martyrs. When one of my fellow missionaries in Italy was hit on his bicycle and killed, the rest of us were in awe that he'd died serving the Lord. Surely, whatever sins the young man had committed, he was now assured the Celestial Kingdom.

As the years passed, though, I began questioning the suffering we all face in life, which seems far too great to serve a useful purpose. If pain and misery are supposed to be a refiner's fire, why do so many people come out of that kiln unrefined? If suffering is supposed to be the most effective teaching tool God can possibly provide, and only a small fraction of us are ever able to improve as a result, I can't help wondering if Mr.You Can Be Perfect Just Like Me! Did poorly in Celestial School.

What do you call someone who graduates last in Godhood class?

A god!

The Book of Mormon tells us that after Christ visited the Americas, the Nephites and Lamanites lived together peacefully for 200 years. They had all things in common, there was no strife, everyone was happy. So does that mean that for 200 years, no one learned a single important lesson? No one suffered enough to qualify for the Celestial Kingdom? All that peace and happiness was for nothing?

If the only way God can teach us the lessons we need is to allow other people to rob, beat, rape, torture, oppress, and kill us, he's either a terribly shitty God *or* those of us trying to be "good" are getting in his way. If people *need* to be robbed, beaten, raped, tortured, oppressed, and killed, treating them kindly is making it *harder* for them to improve their souls.

So which is it to be? God, out of the goodness of his heart, needs humans to commit barbarous atrocities *or* God, out of the shittiness of his heart, doesn't give a damn about our suffering here on Earth one shiblum.

It's a false either/or, I suppose. Another alternative is simply that God doesn't exist and therefore can't care one way or the other, that it's up to us to create a just and merciful society.

How do believing Mormons rationalize the teaching that only the kindest, most loving people make it to the Celestial Kingdom when that behavior essentially means they're only looking out for themselves? Why do we believe that the worst humans, especially apostates who break our hearts, are those who will be cast into Outer Darkness when they're the ones giving their all (their eternal happiness) to help others learn and grow?

As the non-Christian King of Siam pointed out so effectively, "It's a puzzlement."

Even more puzzling is how often I've heard from believing Mormons, even bishops, "If I stopped believing in God, there would be nothing to keep me from stealing and killing."

An odd belief, since atheists don't seem to kill in substantially different numbers than Christians. But even stranger is to recognize their lack of comprehension in the rules God set up. If that bishop did stop believing in God, and did start stealing and killing, he'd only then be helping his fellow embryonic deities return to God's presence.

And yet, with every improvement in character those larval gods make because of the ex-bishop's cruelty, they themselves then drift further from the ability to offer their own ultimate sacrifice. The nicer and more loving they become, the less they commit the atrocities that so benefit their fellow man.

It's not a vicious circle. It's a vicious-loving-vicious-loving cycle.

And *that's* the best God can come up with?

We're taught that in the pre-existence God asked for suggestions on how to help his children. One child said he'd go down and atone for their sins. Another said he'd go down and make everyone be good.

Apparently, no one else offered any suggestions. Too bad, since when we brainstorm, it's rarely the first idea that's the best.

And I have to wonder why God is asking his kids what to do in the first place. They haven't even started their Godhood coursework yet. This is *before* the War in Heaven, after all.

But I have to be grateful for these teachings, I suppose. If they weren't so maddeningly illogical, I wouldn't have been able to grow as much as I have and become the thorn in the side of my former Mormon friends who feel too much pain to associate with me any longer. Thus blessing their lives.

Just for the Outer Darkness of it, though, I wish the next prophet would start teaching something more worthwhile. Maybe about how to eradicate abuse and cruelty altogether. Because if he can't do that, he serves no useful function at all.

And that is *not* a blessing to anyone.

Who Said It Best—Republicans or Democrats?

"All Lives Matter!"

"My Body, My Choice!"

"Believe Women!"

In one episode of the popular television series, *The Big Bang Theory*, Howard teases Raj by asking the gang to guess whom he was addressing when he made various comments—his beloved dog or his beautiful girlfriend. "Emily or Cinnamon?" Howard asks. "'How could such a little girl eat such a big steak?'" The humor stretches throughout the episode as again and again, the gang has trouble deciding who was the intended recipient.

Similarly, as Americans struggle through the pandemic, we hear protesters and activists every day on the news and have a surprisingly difficult time figuring out who made a particular declaration. "All Lives Matter!" Oh, that's the platitude from the right, we remember, when certain white folks try to deny the bias that leads to unprovoked killings of people of color.

But no, this time it was said by someone on the left, urging conservatives not to "restart" the economy too soon, to reconsider their willingness to sacrifice additional tens of thousands of lives—lives of the elderly, diabetics, those with asthma, lives of poor people, ethnic minorities, asylum seekers, and inmates. Lives of medical professionals.

When Republican leaders organize to discuss how many COVID-19 deaths are acceptable, could that be considered a "death panel"?

If "an injustice anywhere is a threat to justice everywhere," does being required to wear a mask in public constitute "injustice"?

We're hearing people at "Liberate our state!" rallies shouting, "My body, my choice!" It's jarring to hear, of course, as only a few months ago, these freedom fighters were enraged when women claimed the same right.

Likewise, it used to be Democrats who insisted we give sexual assault victims a fair hearing when they accuse powerful men. But now it seems they want to brush credible accusations aside when *their* guy faces scrutiny.

Democrats dismiss Fox News as partisan, but if Chris Hayes simply reports on Joe Biden's accuser, there's an immediate call to MSNBC for his dismissal. "He's not supporting Democrats!"

The list goes on, Republicans and Democrats playing "Who wore it best?" on the red carpet of punditry.

"You need to respect the office of the President!"

"We're the ones looking out for your best interests."

"It's the *way* they're protesting that's inappropriate."

Emily or Cinnamon? Like Penny, we find the questions much more difficult than they first appear.

Are those waving Confederate flags patriots or are they traitors?

Do Democrats really believe science if they won't stop supporting fossil fuel corporations?

Is it a cheap shot to call folks waving a swastika at a "reopen" rally Nazis? Is a sign at the rally proclaiming *Arbeit macht frei* truly pro-freedom or is it actually pro-genocide?

I *wish* this game was merely "Republicans or Democrats?" but it seems to have quickly devolved into something far more sinister.

The cultural divide in America has become surreal, creating a Bizarro world like that which confused Elaine Benes on *Seinfeld*. For as long as I can remember, extremists on the far right were hoarding food and guns and ammo, preparing to hunker down and shelter in place when an inevitable global crisis arrived. And yet now, so many of these same people use the weapons they've amassed to demand haircuts. They want to go to the mall. They want chicken wings.

Republicans argue that business should "return to normal" because the stress of staying closed will lead to depression and suicide. Yet they seem to have no problem with a "normal" that requires school children to cower under their desks during active shooter drills. Or, worse, flee actual shooters. But maybe that isn't such a novel position, after all. The truth is that conservative values often sacrifice the innocent.

The residents of Flint get poisoned water so those in power can save money. The poor and those who lose their jobs get no healthcare so that corporations can improve profits. Our groundwater, air, and land are polluted so that the wealthy can become wealthier. Public schools in poor neighborhoods get less money so that children from wealthier areas can maintain their advantage.

All in the name of freedom.

But with freedom like this, who needs oppression?

And oddly, the DNC takes money from all the same corrupting influences. They decry the high price of prescription drugs but only the far left "fringe" raises the idea of universal healthcare. Democrats demand "transparency" from the Trump administration and yet have no problem with Biden refusing access to the records where Tara Reade's official complaint might reside.

When Emily confronts Raj's friends after a day of relentless teasing, she says she loves that her boyfriend is so sweet to both her and the dog. She kisses the likable loser full on the lips in front of his friends as a reward.

And then backs away, her nose wrinkled in disgust as she pulls something off her tongue. "Why do you have dog hair in your mouth?"

Perhaps the problem with understanding the real values of either Republicans or Democrats is that their slogans only serve the underlying function of emotionally appeasing the masses while still directing every resource that matters to those in power.

The game isn't nearly as funny in real life.

Republicans Need to Take Responsibility for Their Actions...and So Do Democrats

Democrats were up in arms over Republicans forcing voters to the polls in Wisconsin during a pandemic. And they were right. What the Republicans did was an outrage. The GOP needs to take responsibility for this atrocity and the many others they commit that destroy lives and livelihoods every day.

But Democrats need to stop blaming Republicans for their own multitude of failures. It's not the GOP's fault that Democrats don't push for fare-free public transit. It's not the GOP's fault that Democrats don't ban fracking. It's not the GOP's fault that Democrats don't demand ranked choice voting.

As a gay man excommunicated by the Mormon Church for coming out, I heard friends and family testify that AIDS was the natural result of sin. Sure, gay men were free to sin if we chose, but we weren't free to escape the consequences of our actions. *We* were responsible for everything bad in our lives.

So I watch in amazement as conservative religious leaders insist on gathering large congregations in the midst of a pandemic. They have freedom of religion, they insist defiantly. Atheists are just trying to persecute them by banning large groups. "Christians aren't afraid of dying," we hear them say.

Most Christian religions, though, frown on suicide. Gambling, too. I would think Russian roulette falls under at least one of those proscriptions.

If aborting a fetus is a mortal sin, isn't it also immoral to behave in a manner known to spread a deadly pathogen? Sure, Pastor Bill didn't put a gun to Grandma's head and pull the trigger, but wouldn't it still be a sin to pour cyanide into a community's water supply, even if he didn't target Grandma specifically?

The Las Vegas shooter wasn't aiming at a specific person. He just sprayed death randomly into the crowd, killing 58 people and injuring hundreds more.

When parents complain about the quality of schools in poor neighborhoods, conservatives accuse them of blaming others for their own circumstances. Poor folks are poor, conservatives say, because they have a bad work ethic, because they don't apply themselves in school, because they waste their money on cell phones. "Society" isn't responsible for the poor, they insist. Conservatives certainly aren't responsible. Poor people have no one to blame but themselves. They need to take responsibility.

And yet conservatives have no problem when President Trump refuses to accept responsibility for any of his administration's failures regarding the pandemic. First, he says the coronavirus isn't a problem. It's being overstated by Democrats who want to attack him. Then he says it *is* a problem, and he's said so all along. Then he says China lied and didn't tell him how serious the problem was. Then he says the problem isn't so bad and he wants to open up businesses and churches by Easter. Then he says we're facing one of the worst crises in our country's history. Then he says the lack of testing and masks and ventilators is the CDC's fault, Obama's fault, the fault of governors, the fault of medical personnel. Then he says he's made sure hospitals have what they need. Then he blames the WHO for not alerting him in time to prevent the virus from becoming a problem in the U.S.

It's always someone else's fault. Conservatives don't believe in taking responsibility for their actions.

They *do* believe, however, that *poor* people are responsible for *their* problems. They believe gay people are responsible. Women impregnated by rapists are responsible. Refugees fleeing violence in their countries of origin are responsible. Students racking up forty thousand dollars in debt are responsible. People who lose their health insurance when their jobs are terminated are responsible.

Corporations, of course, are *not* responsible. Banks aren't responsible. The wealthy aren't responsible.

The Democratic National Committee blames Bernie supporters for Hillary Clinton's loss in 2016. They blame Comey. They blame Putin. They blame the Electoral College. They blame young people who didn't vote. They refuse to accept responsibility for barring Sanders supporters during the primary. Worse, they refuse to accept responsibility for nominating a candidate who wasn't offering what voters wanted. That might not have been Sanders, but it certainly wasn't Clinton.

The DNC's presumptive nominee in 2020 is Joe Biden. If he doesn't win the general election, the DNC will blame Bernie supporters again. They'll blame Russia. They'll blame the Electoral College. They'll blame COVID-19.

Whatever the reason, it *won't* be because they chose to push a lackluster candidate without the vision necessary to solve problems like equal access to healthcare and education. It won't be because they chose not to address systemic racism or tackle the climate crisis head on.

People in recovery learn that they must stop blaming others for the problems in their lives. They must accept their part in those failures. They understand that making amends is part of recovery. And they know they can rely on one another to get through the hard times.

Democrats have no control over what Republicans do or don't do. They only have control over their own choices. If they want to regain power to shape society, they must stop blaming others for their inadequate platform and instead offer the people of this country what they need.

The Democratic Party Can't Be Changed from Within

When leftists complain that liberal Democratic candidates aren't bold enough once in office, we're told that change takes time and is only effective if it comes from within. If these liberals are too bold, they tell us, they can't be insiders and will lose what little power they have. The problem is that they willingly give up their power to be an insider in the first place, securing their own failure from the start.

Elected Democratic leaders keep voting for pandemic relief packages that overwhelmingly benefit corporations at the expense of the people, promising that "next time" they'll insist on a better deal. This behavior, though, pre-dates the pandemic by decades. The public health crisis is just the latest excuse. Liberals and progressives had to vote for this bad deal first to earn the power to say, "*Now* you owe me a favor." But when the next package deal comes up, still overwhelmingly in favor of corporations, our Democratic saviors again vote for it, telling us once more that the "next time" will be different. Even when offering a fake proposal for the following relief bill, Democratic leaders *still* don't include the programs and policies necessary to address real needs, and *this* is in the "showy" package, the one everyone knows will need to be renegotiated before it gets passed. They simply can't be bothered to pretend they care about our priorities.

Even Lucy van Pelt was more convincing when asking Charlie Brown to kick the football.

I was excommunicated from the Mormon Church over thirty years ago for being gay, but for decades I kept writing stories about "progressive" Mormons, hoping that Mormons reading my books would slowly move to the left. Organizations like Affirmation for LGBTQ Mormons tried to work "from the inside" as well. As did Family Fellowship, the Mormon equivalent to PFLAG. Mormons Building Bridges tried a similar approach, as did Mama Dragons. All these organizations, and other writers like myself, tried to effect change "from inside." *Sunstone* magazine has been publishing since 1975, and almost no "active" Mormons have even heard of it.

The problem is that once a Mormon, or worse, an ex-Mormon, says *anything* contrary to official policy, they are automatically seen as outsiders whose words must immediately be discounted. It's *impossible* to change policies on LGBTQ issues from the inside. It's impossible to effect change even on the rights of heterosexual women from the inside. Mormon feminists have been excommunicated for such heresy.

If one day the Mormon Church makes any significant changes, they will *only* come from leaders at the top. I could hang around another thirty years in docile anticipation, but I won't live that long. So I invest my efforts to make the world a better place elsewhere. A remote chance of success is better than none.

Liberal and progressive Democrats will also have a greater chance of success once they realize the same thing applies to them.

Democratic outsiders, the rebels, the troublemakers, are squashed again and again until they are finally offered a tiny bit of power. They're appointed to this committee or that task force, *if* they promise to toe the line. So they do, because they know that this act of compromise will mean Democratic leadership now owes them a favor.

But moral clarity and the strength it provides are what become compromised. In the film version of John Grisham's *The Firm*, Tom Cruise's character is enticed by all the perks he gets from joining a prestigious law firm. He isn't ethically compromised yet, but when the senior partners begin suspecting he won't remain loyal, they set him up with a beautiful woman confiding a heartrending sob story.

The Tom Cruise character has sex with the woman, which is of course all caught on film, and now the firm has leverage against him. If he doesn't do as they say, they'll go to his wife.

When liberal Democrats we've voted for cheat on us, it's not easy to forgive. Especially if they insist on continuing an open relationship without our consent.

I don't want a candidate or elected official to *say* the right things in a speech, no matter how eloquently he or she says it. What matters is the vote. *Every single time*. On a pre-employment integrity test, what's the correct answer for the following question:

You know you could skim a little money from several large accounts without being noticed. Do you

skim the accounts every chance you get?

skim the accounts only twice a year?

skim the accounts once and never again?

enlist someone else to skim the accounts so that your hands are clean?

The answer "None of the above" never seems to be an option in the world of politics. But compromising your ethics can only weaken your ability to command from the moral high ground, never strengthen it.

Not voting for an inadequate relief package when everyday people desperately need *some* relief means you'll get some flak. But haven't any of these "rebels" noticed they're already getting flak every day? They tell us that minimal relief is better than none, so they must get *something* in the hands of the poor immediately. They promise to get us a better deal "next time."

I see Lucy van Pelt holding the football again.

Every single time you vote against the needs of the people in favor of corporations and their owners, you give opponents anywhere on the political spectrum ammunition against you. "So-and-so *says* they're for student loan forgiveness. But look how they voted on this piece of legislation."

Those who hate you, those who have never supported you, won't suddenly support you because you've been broken into submission. They'll stick with the candidates who were on their side from the start. And those who used to believe in you will have lost faith in anything you tell them. Yes, you *say* you've learned your lesson, but I won't know if that's true until *after* the next election. You burned me before. Maybe this other candidate will, too, but if I must take a chance, I'll go with the one who hasn't burned me yet.

There are those on the left who hope that if enough Democrats leave the party, its leaders will realize the error of their ways and change. Who knows? Maybe they will and maybe they won't. But it's pointless to wait. The carrot on the end of a stick never gets any closer.

In the last fifteen to twenty years, Mormons have been leaving their church in droves. And what have Church leaders who see this departure done? Well, they now allow sister missionaries to wear slacks...sometimes. Black members can now wear "black hairstyles" inside the temple. And teenage girls can now hand out towels in the temple, a privilege once denied them. That's all new. Groundbreaking. But leggings for women in their daily lives? No, that's a bridge too far. Women who commit such sin still need to confess to their bishop and repent. Beards for male BYU students? Such a violation of the Honor Code will still get them expelled from college.

I'm not wasting any more time on vain hopes for improvement from within. Not in the Mormon Church and not in the Democratic Party.

Last night, my ex-Mormon husband and I watched *Monsters University*. One throwaway scene near the beginning shows a slug "racing" to his first class. He arrives in the final minute of the film, after the semester is over and everyone else has gone home.

Despite its many flaws, I enjoyed being part of the Mormon Church and hated to leave, especially since so many people I love and respect are still believers. But my life is immeasurably better since. Liberals and progressives need to consider that leaving the Democratic Party may be a more successful path for them as well. The one thing we can be sure of, unfortunately, is that staying won't accomplish anything that's meaningful—because it isn't "time" Democratic leaders need. It's the opportunity to keep supporting their corporate donors.

Do Extremists Just Want to Kill People They Don't Like?

Washington state lawmaker Robert Sutherland (R-Granite Falls) took part in a protest at the state capitol in Olympia, calling for an armed rebellion if he couldn't go fishing as a result of the stay-at-home order. I understand the concern over economic hardship caused by social distancing to slow the pandemic and try to give people the benefit of the doubt in regard to their motivations. But the more I watch how these extremists at "let us get sick and die" protests behave, I think all they're really looking for is a chance to "defend" themselves. Many on the far right have been talking about "second amendment solutions" for years. They don't want to go fishing or go shopping. They want to kill people they hate and are trying to make it look like self-defense.

I think of police officers who shoot unarmed motorists and then plant a gun on the body. I think of "good neighbors" who start a fight with someone "suspicious" and then "have" to kill that person in self-defense. Yes, not all officers are horrible. Not all neighbors are wannabe killers. But some are. And the evidence accumulates daily that these extremists who want to "liberate Minnesota" and "liberate Michigan" and "liberate the country" are driven more by hatred than the desire to see a movie at the theater.

If all you want is to see a movie, why are you waving a Confederate flag while you protest? If all you want is to go bowling, why are you shoving and beating journalists who are simply recording you exercising your First Amendment rights? If all you want is to go fishing, why are you threatening to kill your colleagues at work?

I'll admit, there are some people on the far right who I don't like, a few I might actually hate. But I don't spend my days coming up with ways to justify killing them. I hope to reason. I hope to persuade. I hope to rally enough voters who are open to reason and persuasion to vote. But I don't look for opportunities to kill.

When it first became apparent that ICE detention centers were going to be overrun by the virus, concerned citizens began demanding that asylum seekers be released. But I knew it was never going to happen. Those on the right might never say it publicly, but many of them are *happy* the families they've put in concentration camps are going to die. Some will act deeply offended and scream their denial, the way they pretend Trump was only joking about shooting up bleach. We all know the truth, but we're pressured into believing we've signed a social contract to keep pretending we don't. So even if the offensive comment is true, perhaps "civility" dictates an apology on my part.

The same civility that has right-wing politicians keeping people imprisoned as the virus spreads through the camps. Sure, a few children are released, a few parents are deported, but tens of thousands of human beings remain trapped as the infection spreads.

"Leaders" throughout the country are also "working on" ways to release non-violent offenders from state and federal prisons. And as they "try" to "work out" the details, the infection rate at some prisons has already reached 75%.

Because really, though no decent person would say so out loud, this virus is serendipitous, a *perfect* way to get rid of so many people those on the right don't like.

You know, like the black and brown people in major cities—and on reservations—who die in disproportionately high numbers. Sure, we'll get around to providing tests and ventilators and treatment eventually, but let's allow the riff raff to die off first. We can just say it took longer than we'd hoped to get ourselves organized. Better yet, it was those stupid Democratic governors who couldn't get their act together. If anyone's to blame, it's *them*.

Anne Frank wasn't "murdered" during the Holocaust. She died of typhus, as did her sister Margot. Was it really the fault of their captors that these teenage girls got sick? Disease is simply a part of life, after all.

It's hardly natural, though, if you deliberately create the conditions where the disease can kill those you don't like in massive numbers.

People say that love is blind. But it turns out that hate is blind, too. Some of these extremists are so driven by their hatred they can't grasp the fact that many of the people they love will also die because of their actions.

The right-wing lieutenant governor of Texas said, "There are more important things than living." And he's right, at least as far as these extremists are concerned. And that more important thing…is killing.

I only hope that for the rest of us, there are more important things than complaining. Or pretending.

Like organizing, striking, protesting. And voting.

Politics as Religious Conviction

The religious right is ramping up for a modern-day crusade. That's not a metaphor. Racially motivated killings are in the news every day. Homophobic and transphobic murders are committed regularly. Poor men and women are forced to work in conditions that *will* kill a significant portion of them. When the first few drops of rain fall on a sidewalk during a thunderstorm, we initially see individual wet spots before us, but the dry spaces between them shrink rapidly, and after only a few minutes, the entire surface is covered. We don't need to conduct a violent pre-emptive strike to acknowledge the urgency of making political change while we can. Every election is touted as the "most important" of our lifetime. We're trained to dismiss such claims as emotional manipulation, which they often are, but the danger we face now isn't theoretical. It's real and growing stronger every day.

Last night, I watched Henry Gates on PBS as he revealed the fate of the extended families of Jeff Goldblum, Terry Gross, and Marc Maron during WWII. The phrase I kept hearing was, "and that's when further details vanished from the record" as each family's community was obliterated, one after the other. The program airing afterward told the story of the Pittsburgh synagogue where 11 worshippers were killed, just days after their latest active shooter training. I watched a

---

survivor of the Jewish deli shooting in Paris take a self-defense course while the widow of one of those murdered happily recounted her courtship and marriage. She seemed surprisingly well-adjusted, till the moment in the story where she had to talk about that terrible day.

Yet perhaps the worst segment of the program was the summary of how a former hero, a Holocaust survivor who rose to extreme wealth and then donated almost 80% of his fortune to charitable organizations, was recast as an evil Jew trying to take over the world. George Soros was turned into a scapegoat in Hungary so a dictator could consolidate power.

Then I watched as the Labour Party in the UK embraced anti-Semitism, pushing its many Jewish liberals out of the party.

As I watched these disturbing events onscreen, my husband sat in his office in the rear of the house, enjoying a weekly Zoom meeting with friends. After rejoining me in the living room, he told me that a group of racists had hacked into their gathering, shouting the N-word over and over until the one black woman in attendance signed out. After several minutes, the admins regained control and blocked the intruders, but the incident left everyone shaken. It was hardly the first time the black member of the group had faced such language. It was just the first time some of the white folks in the group had felt they were under attack as well.

As ex-Mormons, my husband and I were both raised to believe blacks were morally inferior, that they'd been "less valiant in the pre-existence before we came to Earth." Even now, *decades* after we left the Church, when we see a black driver ignoring a crosswalk or a black pedestrian tossing a piece of trash on the sidewalk, for a split second, maybe only half a second, we think, "What can you expect from someone like that?" Many of us who are happily ex-Mormon have moved past the unhealthy lessons we've been taught, yet even hearing current LDS leaders insist all people are equal regardless of the color of their skin doesn't *entirely* erase all the former teachings still clinging tightly to the neurons that code our memories and deepest beliefs.

How much worse is it for those who are still trained every day by their religious leaders to consider any other group of humans "less than"?

The latest killing of an unarmed black man by the police in Minneapolis was all over Facebook the past couple of days, yet not a single person in my family commented on the death of George Floyd. One family member several years ago had posted "Police Lives Matter!" in response to a previous incident, but other than that, I've seen nothing posted in regard to any of the dozens of killings that have made it into the news since then. My relatives live in the Deep South, where I grew up as well. I remember my parents buying me a Confederate cap and a rebel flag to play with when we visited the Civil War memorials in Vicksburg, where at least one of my ancestors had fought. My mother would say, "Skip this monument. These are Yankees. Oh, here's a good one. One of *ours*."

My mother was a genuinely wonderful person in almost every way. But she was infected by the hatred she'd been taught her entire life. When we describe those folks saying and doing racist things as bigots, however accurate the label, they are *unable* to see themselves or each other as such because what they *can* see is that they're "nice" people in so many other ways. You know, the "fine" people at the rally in Charleston who chanted "Blood and soil!" as they marched with other neo-Nazis while a young woman was murdered by another right-wing extremist.

Most of my religious friends treated me wonderfully…until the day they learned I was gay.

But these right-wing folks are all on the "same side," so they treat *each other* well, they're nice to *each other*, they're "good people" in their own and each other's eyes. We're angry when they demonize us, but they are just as angry when we demonize them, because they honestly cannot see the harm and suffering they cause.

Is that really possible?

The evidence before us suggests that it is.

A vegetarian might well worry about the pain steak lovers cause the animals they slaughter, but do vegetarians consider the possibility a plant might not enjoy being chopped down and eaten, either? Perhaps a plant isn't truly able to feel pain the way animals do, but the point is that we don't even consider the possibility. It's simply not part of our mindset. Does that mean we're heartless and cruel to cucumbers?

Of course, our *absence* of concern for the feelings of vegetables isn't the same as the *presence* of a powerful animosity toward others that often exists in the hearts of the religious right.

The Civil War isn't ancient history for people in the South. Many white folks have passed on their anger, generation after generation, at having lost the battle to keep their slaves. Their anger isn't only over losing the war, the way a petulant child might be upset over a game of checkers. The loss is an overwhelming message sent directly into the deepest reaches of their psyche that they aren't superior to blacks as they'd claimed. That idea of superiority is such a core belief that losing it is like hearing you're a pod person from *Invasion of the Body Snatchers.* "No! *They're* the pod people! *I'm* human! I'm one of the good guys! I *am*!"

They tell themselves this every day, every time they see a news story about a black criminal, every time they see a black person in public say something "rude," every time they hear rap music. In many ways, their behavior is the same as that of news anchors who every single day point out something awful Trump has said, concluding with, "Can we now all finally agree that Trump is terrible?" The possibility that even one person in the audience isn't yet convinced threatens their conclusion, and they *must* believe they are right. So they spend every day "proving" their point over and over and over again.

Such emotional neediness is unappealing no matter who is doing it, but right now, most of the physical danger is coming from those on the right. If a black person does better in life than they have, it's because the black person received an unfair advantage. If a Jew does better, it's because there's a secret Jewish underground. No one who isn't a white Christian should be doing *better* than they are. If someone is, it can only be because he's stolen what rightfully belongs to whites. And thieves must be punished.

This incredible lack of self-confidence may seem pathetic or even laughable, but the desperation and simmering anger it creates is real, and it's being stoked by the unscrupulous to gain power. And just as a virus doesn't recognize borders, neither does hatred. It has spread to every region of our nation. White supremacist groups exist even in the most liberal states.

In the wake of the most recent police killing, a black church was burned in Mississippi, with the words "Vote Trump" spray-painted on the brick wall outside. Of course, we all know Mississippi isn't a liberal state. We *expect* this kind of thing in the south.

That's a problem. This isn't a "new" normal *there*. We cannot allow it to become normal everywhere.

White protesters armed with assault weapons rallied in Minnesota at the capitol recently to protest stay-at-home orders yet faced no repercussions. When unarmed men and women gathered to protest the unprovoked killing of George Floyd, they were met with riot gear and tear gas.

Even now, with a photo of the police officer kneeling on George Floyd's neck until he suffocated to death posted next to a photo of Colin Kaepernick kneeling in protest before a football game, I see empathy-challenged people insisting, "Two wrongs don't make a right," as if killing someone and protesting the killing are not only equal, but also both wrong.

Yet those actions *are* equal to them. If a black person has "attitude," he deserves to be killed. Not shunned. Not chastised. Not fired. *Killed.* An equal response to the "offense." And the very *existence* of blacks, gays, Jews, Muslims, Native Americans, and many others is the offense that cannot be forgiven.

The violence isn't caused merely by a few crazy people on the fringe. It's perpetrated and perpetuated by those in uniform and elected officials in office. It's the institutions themselves that are problematic, as well as all the "regular folks" who accept these killings as "understandable." Most of my right-wing friends and family aren't actively committing these atrocities. They simply don't care a great deal if they happen. Even those who feel the police did "something" wrong have a hundred priorities higher on their list.

Like same-sex marriage. And atheists. And people saying some of the most dreaded words in the English language: Happy Holidays!

And, of course, the abortion doctors who "murder" millions of babies. Because to the religious right, there is *no difference* between a fertilized egg, a zygote, a morula, a blastocyst, an embryo, a fetus, and a baby. Explaining the science is meaningless. They *know* anyone who doesn't agree with them is a murderer. Murderers, clearly, should be put to death. And while there may be no difference between a zygote and a newborn baby, there's *plenty* of difference between a murderer and an executioner.

This isn't a case of semantics. It's not theory. It's *truth* to them, and someone who bases their decisions and behavior on these kinds of truths are left with few options.

If *you* had to vote for either a repulsive man who fondles women and makes fun of the disabled *or* an intelligent woman with no known scandals *but* who will install judges who ensure that millions of babies will be not "aborted" but *murdered*, what *to you* is the lesser of two evils?

We like to call those on the religious right hypocrites, and certainly many of them are, just as many are on the left (shout-out to the latest "Karen" in Central Park), but in the mindset of a religious conservative, these two candidates aren't even close. One is bad and the other is very, very, very, *very* bad.

Unfortunately, "understanding" where they're coming from doesn't eliminate the danger we face. If anything, it helps us realize we're not worrying about a non-existent threat.

A man in the Reopen North Carolina protest said he was willing to kill to fight against the New World Order, and that such killings of fellow Americans wasn't terrorism. For most right-wing protesters, it's the unquestionable will of God.

They *mean* it.

In my Baptist high school, we used to sing, "God said it. I believe it. That settles it for me."

Rolling our eyes is not an appropriate response. Almost all of us make fun of these extremists, even knowing it's counterproductive. I do it, too. It's difficult not to. But these devout believers are serious about their convictions, and they've become more and more emboldened over the past few years.

To paraphrase Condoleezza Rice, "We don't want the smoking gun to be a mushroom cloud over the ACLU." Over a Jewish community center. Over a gay nightclub.

When people tell us they hate us, we should take their word for it.

At a neighborhood park a few days ago, while admiring the beautiful rhododendrons and brilliant hummingbirds, I could also hear the repeated "bam bam bam bam" from a police association shooting range nearby. It's a sound I hear from my front porch every day, something I never quite get used to. Since I live across the street from a school, I dread the day I might hear that sound from twenty yards away. When my husband attends far-left political meetings a few neighborhoods over, I worry about the sirens I hear in the distance.

Two elderly women chatted with me at this neighborhood park last week, from a reasonable distance, about how most people were being pleasant and cooperative in the effort to keep the park safe. When they saw a couple of people blocking the path to take pictures, the women waited patiently for them to finish. Then a man in the group turned to the women and held out his phone. "Would you take a picture of us?"

The women deferred, saying they'd rather not risk infection. The man, who'd been friendly a moment before, now saw them as enemies and hissed, "For something that's no worse than the flu!?"

The women, both elderly, were shocked. "People die of the flu," one of them said. "And even if you don't die, it's miserable. So even *if* COVID were no worse, I wouldn't want it."

But the man was furious, enraged, full of immediate, irrational hatred.

It's become a religious conviction for those on the right that Democrats are using the coronavirus as an excuse to deprive Republicans of their liberty. We're not talking politics anymore—we're talking religion. And when someone feels they're morally superior, that others are morally inferior, and that God wants the righteous to destroy his enemies…well, let's just say *Where Angels Go, Trouble Follows*.

As a Mormon missionary, I felt I had been called as a *Saturday's Warrior*, chosen to "gather the faithful" in the

Last Days. Those of us sent to Rome talked about the awesome responsibility of being sent to "Satan's doorstep." A friend who was assigned to Portland just months after Mt. St. Helens erupted felt thankful that Heavenly Father had prepared the sinners in that area by "sending them a message."

I was shocked to discover that one of my missionary colleagues was a Democrat. Of course, he'd converted to the true church as an adult. He didn't know any better. Still, I thought, it was surprising he'd been found worthy to serve a mission.

Months later, another missionary colleague suffered a nervous breakdown. When we knocked on doors and the occupants of the apartment would tell us calmly they weren't interested in our message, my companion would turn to me after the door closed and address me as if I were the occupant. "You're not interested!? Not interested in your own salvation!? You're not interested in being with your family after you die!? Not interested in following the Savior!?"

I had learned by this time not to take rejection personally. If people were interested, great, we'd teach them. If they weren't, that was their decision. I didn't need a complete stranger to validate my life.

But my companion did. He took a stranger's disinterest in his religion as a *personal affront*. An affront to his intelligence, an affront to his two-year sacrifice, and an affront to God himself. This emotional reaction was so severe he was barely able to function.

I know two men who ended their friendship because one thought Daniel Craig was a great James Bond and the other thought he was ugly.

But what's happening in politics isn't funny, it isn't "stupid." It's not "worrisome."

By their very nature, political parties are opponents. What's changed in the last few decades is the growing conversion of politics into religion. It's deadly enough when one Christian religion demonizes another—think of the Reformation in Europe, the Spanish Inquisition, and the situation in Ireland. But when Republicans see Democrats *literally* as the party of the Devil, it's not just ridiculous. It's *dangerous*.

An elected official in New Mexico recently announced, "The only good Democrat is a dead Democrat." A police officer in Louisiana bemoaned the fact that more blacks hadn't died in the pandemic. These aren't just "feelings" and "opinions." They are votes. They are policies.

They are gun owners.

When someone says they want you dead, believe them.

For the religious right, gays were responsible for Hurricane Katrina. Gays and Jews were responsible for 9/11. Gays and Jews and Bill Gates are responsible for COVID. Except, of course, when the Chinese are responsible.

In the mid-1990s, I converted to Judaism and was active in the community for several years. It's been a long while since I identified as a Jew (I see myself as a Mormon Jewish atheist) but I remembered my time as a Jew fondly and kept two mezuzot affixed to the door frames of my bedroom and office. I never nailed one on the front doorpost, always aware that announcing Jewish affiliation could be problematic. It's the same reason I never pasted pro-gay bumper stickers on my car.

A few months ago, I removed the two mezuzot inside my home. It's not that I'm "afraid to stand up" for the Jews any more than I'm afraid to stand up for gays or any other oppressed group or person. I simply realize we're not in a period of "rude" discourse. Right-wing politicians have been pushing hatred for so many years that now, with the pandemic providing more fuel, this nation has become a drought-stricken, desiccated forest.

Maybe *most* people of every political persuasion are good, but it only takes one idiot to toss a lit cigarette into the brush. And once that conflagration begins, we'll all be caught up in the disaster that follows.

We see the irrationality of those on the right every day but don't want to accuse anyone of plotting our literal destruction. It might "raise tensions" or "lower the level of civility." And just as some whites can't entertain the horrifying notion that they might not be superior to others, the rest of us find it too frightening to consider that our lives might legitimately be at risk. So we convince ourselves that this is all rhetoric and policy, quite bad enough though not cataclysmic.

Then last night, I heard Terry Gross wonder if she would have known when to leave if she had lived in eastern Europe just before the outbreak of WWII. Would she have gotten out? "When's the right time?" she asked.

It's not a rhetorical question.

In *The Day after Tomorrow*, the character played by Dennis Quaid urges the scientist played by Ian Holm, "It's time you got out of there."

The scientist replies sadly, "I'm afraid that time has come and gone, my friend."

For better or for worse, we're here and we're not going anywhere. Let's do what we can to help each other survive.

I sat on my porch this morning so I could listen to the bees buzzing about the California lilac.

But all I could hear was gunfire from the shooting range somewhere on the far side of the park.

Back Yard Politics is Destroying America

What happens when "Not in my back yard!" turns into "Not in my country!"?

No one wants a garbage dump in their community. The most "law and order" people among us don't want a prison in their neighborhood. The most humane don't want a homeless encampment in theirs. No one, rich or poor, liberal or conservative, wants an oil pipeline or fracking well a quarter mile from home. This natural self-interest has always been problematic, as the privileged ensure their own comfort while foisting the unpleasant side effects of our culture on the most vulnerable.

But what happens when the "toxic waste" voters don't want anywhere near them includes people with dark skin? What happens when it includes LGBTQ folks, refugees, immigrants, people who worship differently? Most importantly, what happens when the leaders these voters elect follow through on the unspoken truth they've heard loud and clear—America's "back yard" is the entire country, and there's *no* acceptable place anywhere in our nation for those they consider human trash?

People with a conscience can't allow themselves to actively "eliminate" people they deem unacceptable...but they *can* rationalize voting for someone who will do it for them. "No one's perfect," they say, "and he has other policies I like." But they're not particularly worried when Japanese Americans are interred in concentration camps, when AIDS sweeps through gay communities, when Indigenous women are raped and murdered in record numbers. They're OK with COVID-19 disproportionately killing blacks. If Latinx families are separated, imprisoned in dangerous conditions, and eventually deported back to even more dire circumstances, it's no concern of theirs.

What happens when a majority of Americans, or at least a majority in states most privileged by the Electoral College, *want* all these groups to "go away"?

We keep telling ourselves that *our* country could never devolve into fascism and dictatorship. But then we creep ever closer to Argentina's corruption of the late 1970s and early 80s, when up to 30,000 dissidents and human rights activists "disappeared."

We all want to live in Utopia. Mormons tried out the United Order, a Finnish man in Brazil created Fazenda Penedo, and Jim Jones established Jonestown. Some of the more than three dozen American experiments were more successful than others, but even when we see failure after failure, we keep trying because we all want something better than we have now. Even the most privileged among us, who should already have everything they want, still want more. This longing is not just a personal or cultural need; it's almost certainly rooted in our DNA.

But whatever its source, one thing that history has shown us time and again is that oppressing, imprisoning, and exterminating those we see as obstacles to our idea of Utopia is never the solution.

We worry that elections are useless, that there is widespread voter suppression and voter fraud, that paper ballots are destroyed, that voting machines are rigged or hacked. We worry that even if the candidate we choose ends up winning, in the end it will make no difference that is both meaningful and positive.

We can be sure, though, that *not* voting *will* make a difference, an extraordinarily meaningful one, and it most definitely won't be positive.

Both intellectual and human purges are deadly, even when in support of lofty ideals.

Whatever our personal goals for the best life we can lead, each of us should want to cleanse from the neighborhood we call America all elected officials who consider other humans, even many of their own supporters, as no more than troublesome weeds infesting their dictatorial back yard.

We must remember that remaining "neutral" by abstaining always favors the oppressor. Let's commit to vote so we can clean up our neglected front yard.

Does Anybody Here Know
How to Fly a Plane?

On April 28, 1988, Aloha Airlines Flight 243 lost 18 feet of its roof in mid-flight, killing a flight attendant who was sucked out of the plane, and seriously injuring another flight attendant and seven passengers. An additional 60 passengers sustained minor injuries. Pilot Robert Schornstheimer, a former flight instructor, had created simulator exams for his students that encompassed multiple crises. A few students complained that so many things would never go wrong at the same time in real life. But Schornstheimer and his co-pilot, Madeline Tompkins, faced more than immediate decompression of the plane and the loss of the cockpit door. The noise of rushing wind was so loud they had to communicate through hand signals. They were unable to reach the one flight attendant still conscious, who was also unable to contact them. The horizontal stabilizers were seriously damaged, the vertical stabilizer partially damaged along with both wings. They were unable to deploy full flaps upon their emergency landing, forced to attempt the landing at a higher speed than normal. And they were unable to confirm if the landing gear at the nose of the plane had descended or locked into place.

The two pilots landed the plane successfully, such an astonishing feat that it was later turned into the movie

Miracle Landing. As I watch the multiple crises facing America now, hanging on for dear life as I stare at the gaping hole where a protective roof used to be, I remember what happened over the Hawaiian Islands that day in 1988, and I feel a glimmer of hope. A competent pilot can get us through this seemingly impossible ordeal safely.

Oh, wait.

And now I remember another film, *United 93.* Hijackers have taken over the flight. The passengers hear from their loved ones by cell phone what's been happening at the Pentagon and the World Trade Center. They know that if they have any chance at all to survive, they must take over the plane. They form a team, arming themselves with soda cans and whatever else they can find, a beverage cart, their courage, and their determination. They rush the cockpit.

And as they fight the hijackers for the controls, we see through the front window the green grass of a field in Shanksville, Pennsylvania approaching nearer and nearer.

Every time I watch the film, I keep rooting for the passengers. Maybe this time they'll succeed.

For some emotional relief, I watch *Airplane* and am struck by how often the nightly news makes me feel I'm living an absurdist comedy.

Whichever scenario we're facing in our nation today, we must remember that the conclusion isn't determined yet. Stowaway Helen Hayes could still live. Flight attendant Karen Black might manage to avoid the top of the mountain. Pilot Jack Lemmon might reach the surface of the ocean to call for help. We might be able to stand on the wings in the freezing Hudson River long enough to be rescued. If we aren't forced to eat our dead friends while trapped in the Andes.

Perhaps we should see ourselves as the crew of *Apollo 13*. If we can all work together, overcoming personality conflicts and lack of resources to repair the damage, we can still splash down safely and return to our families once again.

Maybe we'll even get to have attractive actors portray us one day in the film version of *Miracle Democracy*.

What if the Current Administration is only the Warm-up Act?

Ever since I came out as gay in the 1980s, I've kept my passport up to date. I always understood that LGBTQ folks had little security, that I might have to flee at a moment's notice. All forms of gay sex were felonies in Louisiana back then. And I knew it was a rare oppressor who made an appointment for the exact hour he was coming to arrest you.

On August 27, 2005, I discovered I had thirty minutes to pack. Because I'd been distracted with the other turmoil in my life—my husband had just died of cancer, I'd been forced to find another place to live, and I'd been transferred at work to a new location I didn't like under a new manager who enjoyed assigning busywork—I hadn't paid much attention to the storm brewing in the Gulf of Mexico. But now Katrina was a Category 5, and I needed to leave immediately.

I grabbed my prescriptions, two changes of clothing, my resumé, and my passport. Then I headed out of town.

I never saw my apartment again.

In December of 2019, I sent an email to a Canadian bank. "What would I need to open an account?" I figured it might not be a bad idea, given the deteriorating political climate in the U.S., to put a thousand dollars aside in another country…just in case. It turned out I'd need a Canadian-issued ID. I hated the idea of traveling to Canada just to get the ID, which would almost certainly not be processed on the spot, requiring me to make a separate trip later to open the bank account.

And I was embarrassed to tell anyone I was making this contingency plan. I might be a hypochondriac, but I didn't want to be a drama queen, too.

So a few more weeks passed. Inertia isn't only a principle of physics. It's also true in psychology. Still, I knew I couldn't put it off *too* long. The von Trapp family escaped Austria *one day* before the border closed. I remembered the harrowing ordeal Betty Mahmoody faced escaping Iran with her daughter, the horrors of the Underground Railroad in the American South, the East Germans killed trying to get across the Berlin Wall. And I couldn't forget the terrifying ordeal a Czech circus troupe endured escaping over a bridge into Bavaria. Hell, even in the wake of Katrina, black New Orleanians were stopped at gunpoint when crossing the Mississippi River Bridge to reach dry land.

Then news about the novel coronavirus started popping up. Boarding a bus to Canada might be risky now. I was already worried about taking public transportation every day, but at least I wasn't in close quarters for three full hours with a potentially contagious seatmate. Perhaps after things died down, I could finally take care of the new account. With mainstream media campaigning against

Sanders and even Warren, the hope of defeating Trump in November seemed less and less likely. I looked up some bus and train schedules, debating how to broach the subject with my husband, who hated using money frivolously.

Then the pandemic hit in full force. I lost one of my part-time jobs and was in danger of losing the other. Had I already waited too long to establish my contingency plan?

A few days later, the border closed.

Since then, the political atmosphere in the U.S. has only grown more volatile. Protesters with promoting White Supremacy, with signs asking for "fags" to be killed, started rallying in public and posting threats online. Trump ramped up taunts against reporters. Hate crimes, already on the rise, increased even more. Protesting fossil fuel projects became felonies. Convicted Trump associates began being released from prison. Trump and Pompeo seemed to be pushing the country toward war with Iran. I realized that if the presidential election was "postponed" in November, or if its results were tossed out, democracy in this country wouldn't survive. It may already be too seriously injured to recover. Investigators and department heads and inspectors general have been dropping like flies for the past three years, and not from a virus.

Though corruption is contagious. As is fear.

Perhaps we've all waited too long to act.

But if any of us makes a comparison to Hitler or the Nazis, we're instantly shamed for doing so, our arguments automatically dismissed as hyperbole. Trump's a buffoon, we're told, not a mastermind. But people *are* dying. They *are* being locked up. People *are* losing everything, and that all started well before the first case of COVID-19. Stalin might be a less problematic example of dictatorship, but too few Americans know enough of the details for the comparison to be effective. Even fewer are aware of the atrocities committed during China's cultural revolution.

Years ago, when I first accepted the permanence of my sexual orientation, I understood that instead of coming out publicly, I could lead a secret life, not letting anyone at church know, not letting my family and straight friends know, not letting anyone at work know. But I already grasped the emotional damage such a life would inflict. While I realize everyone's situation is different, my choice was to tell *everyone*. I wrote letters to politicians, to Church headquarters in Salt Lake, to my local newspaper. I wanted to make sure I was on the FBI's list so that if things ever did get worse for gays, I'd know I couldn't "pass" but would have to fight.

This was the period when senators in DC were suggesting people with HIV be quarantined permanently from the rest of society. Right-wing pundits were demanding gay men be tattooed. Tens of thousands of people were dying because it was "inappropriate" to spend "tax dollars" on HIV research.

As a Mormon, I'd grown up with the concept of a "year's supply." We were routinely taught there would be hard times ahead and we needed to be prepared. At the Baptist high school I attended, we were taught about the

Rapture and its accompanying seven years of tribulation. The message of future crisis was a dominant part of my upbringing. That was almost certainly one of my motivations for reading Holocaust literature as a teen. I wanted to prepare myself emotionally for what lay ahead.

I was going to be one of the survivors.

A rabbi once told me the Shoah could never happen in America.

I'm no longer a believer in any god. But I remember an Auschwitz survivor from the synagogue I attended. I remember the Rwandan genocide. I remember the "disappeared" from Argentina. I remember that one of my high school classmates was a huge fan of David Duke. Every year, I can see the steady increase in gerrymandering, voter purges, elimination of polling stations. I see reports of "glitches" that shift every vote for a Democrat into a vote for a Republican. I see how easily many of my religious family members dismiss police killings of unarmed blacks. Despite slanted coverage by the media, I can see what's been happening to Palestinians my whole life, can see what's happening in Syria right now, can see what's happening to African refugees in overcrowded boats off Italian shores.

After relocating to Seattle in the aftermath of Katrina, I eventually found a decent job as a bank teller. One day, a woman came up to deposit a check into an account for the Freedom Socialist Party. I was a little unnerved as she threw in some casual but clearly proselytory remarks about socialism while I conducted the transaction. I'd heard my entire life how awful socialism was, and although I'd already moved from Republican to Democrat to progressive, this pro-Trotsky indoctrination made me uneasy.

And the woman kept coming back to conduct more business. She was pleasant enough, though, and even invited me to a Christmas party at her home. Having been unable to make many friends in the seven years since I'd arrived in Seattle, I decided to attend with my husband. The activist had mentioned she might need some carpentry work done, and my carpenter husband needed the work.

He ended up joining the FSP, and I began attending occasional events with him down at "the Hall." I did temp work with Radical Women, a group that also met in the same location. I proofed articles for the *Freedom Socialist* newspaper. I took part in some rallies and protests.

And every time I did any of these things, I knew my participation was being recorded by *someone.*

I can't write legibly enough anymore to keep a handwritten journal, so I type it in a Word document. Yet if I save a copy to myself in an email, the next day, I start seeing ads pop up on Facebook for something I've never discussed with anyone, that I've only ever mentioned in my journal. The idea of every communication being examined seems preposterous, but at the very least, attached documents are being scanned for keywords, most likely by corporations, not "the government" (though I admit the distinction is fuzzy). One time, I didn't even write anything anywhere, only had a brief discussion with my husband in the living room during a commercial break in the show we were watching. And two hours later, ads and articles about the subject started popping up on the sidebar in my email. These weren't generic, popular topics. These were targeted ads.

Whenever I talk on the phone, whenever I shoot an email to a friend, whenever I look up something online for a story or essay I'm writing, I'm aware it's all being tracked.

I'm not a fan of conspiracy theories, despite my evangelical upbringing. A friend of mine has suffered for the past thirty years with schizophrenia. I understand enough about delusion to question myself.

But just as we're shamed not to compare the growing fascism in our country with Nazism, we're gaslighted from believing we're being monitored. The story set in East Germany, *The Lives of Others*, could never happen *here*.

The Mormon Church keeps files on dissidents or, as they label us, "apostates." I know members who were assigned to keep tabs on other members. I remember the spies sent to record license plates outside of gay bars in Salt Lake, the students coerced to submit to electroshock "therapy" or be kicked out of school.

When President Trump announced during a press briefing recently that he was taking hydroxychloroquine, my husband suggested Trump's doctors were probably only *telling* him that's what he was taking so he'd shut up about it. I joked that maybe his doctors were secretly the ones pushing it on him just so they could legally administer something that might trigger a heart attack.

And as soon as I said it, I thought, "Will I be arrested now for 'threatening' the president? In my own home, in a private conversation? From a completely powerless position?"

Perhaps not every worry we have these days is justifiable, but I do wonder if it's already too late to save ourselves from the next round of concentration camps and mass murder. Sobibor and Manzanar and Wounded Knee and the killing fields of Cambodia aren't fables and myths from the distant past. And more articles appear every day warning of the growing threat of the extreme far right.

When I was young, I made plans for how I might survive when things "got bad."

I've had to accept that I'm not going to survive.

But I want Mayim Bialik to survive. And I want David Hogg to live. And Melissa Harris-Perry. And the neighbors who stand six feet outside my front door and ask if my husband and I need them to pick anything up for us at the store.

Donald Trump cannot be re-elected. In our dysfunctional two-party system, the Democratic nominee becomes our only viable choice. We can stick with Biden or work in the remaining time before the Democratic convention to push another nominee. We can debate the best strategy, but we need to acknowledge that an oppressive leader doesn't always spark a "revolution."

Sometimes, he and his oppressive successors just continue oppressing...for decades, even centuries.

Like many others, I want to tune out, stop watching the news, hunker down, and try to survive emotionally during this stressful time. But that's exactly what allows ruthless people to gain power. We need to work on saving our democracy as if our lives depend on it. Because one way or another, they do.

Section Seven: COVID

COVID-19 Isn't My First Pandemic

I'm 58 and overweight, with diabetes and high cholesterol. This puts me in a high-risk category for COVID-19. But even those in the most vulnerable populations still have a 90% chance of survival. If we get the virus at all. Having lived through the AIDS crisis of the 1980's and 90's, where the mortality rate was close to 100%, I'm not particularly worried. As a character in one of my favorite 1980's movies, *Tootsie*, said, "Don't-don't-don't-don't panic."

Virtually every gay man my age has lost multiple friends and lovers. In our twenties and thirties, we checked the obituaries in the newspaper every morning. We watched friend after friend go blind, or develop dementia, or grow lesions, and die slow, miserable deaths. Death was a daily part of our life for years. But we went to work, we asked guys out on dates, we went to funerals, and we kept on living.

The Seattle Art Museum recently housed a special collection from the Capodimonte Museum in Naples. Having worked as a Mormon missionary in central and southern Italy, I wanted to experience part of that life again. In addition to the spectacular artwork, I was intrigued by a notecard accompanying one of the paintings. It mentioned that between 1656 and 1658, the bubonic plague wiped out almost 60% of Naples, nearly 150,000 people.

And you know what? The city survived.

In all, the bubonic plague wiped out roughly a third of the world's population in the Middle Ages and in later outbreaks. But life went on.

My grandfather caught the "Spanish flu" in 1918 and was deathly ill for several days. But he survived.

It's societal disruption that will be the larger issue. A native New Orleanian, my life was upended by Hurricane Katrina. Cell phones and the internet were down for weeks. Electricity was out for over a month in most places, sometimes several months. Pumps at gas stations don't work if there's no electricity. Washing machines don't work, either, and when you're cleaning up debris in 95-degree weather, you want to be able to wash your clothes.

A coworker in New Orleans committed suicide after losing everything. I never saw some of my friends again. I lost most of my belongings. I lost my job. I was forced to relocate thousands of miles away and start over. But you know what? I did. Life went on.

Panic will be an even larger issue. At the height of the AIDS crisis, people who were merely suspected of being gay, much less of having the virus, were fired from their jobs. They were kicked out of their apartments with no warning, their belongings dumped on the street.

When I told my grandmother, a rural Mississippi farmer, that I was gay, she wrote to her senators asking them to support gay rights. But she was afraid to hug me.

Disease has swept through human populations for millennia and will continue to do so as long as our species continues to share the planet with bacteria and viruses. Which means for the rest of human existence.

So let's take precautions. Let's wash our hands. Let's cover our coughs and sneezes. Let's stay home from work if we're sick. Let's push for universal healthcare, since the health of the poor and uninsured affects the health of everyone else, too. And the poor and uninsured deserve a fighting chance at life regardless, even apart from pandemics.

It's awful to be sick. And it's heartbreaking to lose loved ones. That's going to happen, though, regardless of COVID-19. My mother died of leukemia at 43. My husband died of liver cancer. A friend was stabbed to death by a gay basher. Premature death of any kind is genuinely tragic. But let's calm down and realize most of us will get through this.

I've already lived through a global pandemic. So have most of you. Let's take a deep breath and remember that the overwhelming majority of us will do so again. And again. And again.

Borrowed Emergency

The temperature was 43 degrees in the Japanese Garden. Rain fell heavily all morning, rare for Seattle, where the precipitation most people complained about was often no more than a light drizzle. This early in the season, only a week after opening at the beginning of March, the rich, vibrant green of all the mosses on our trees and rocks and bridges was the most impressive feature of the park.

Three middle-aged women walked up to my window on their way out of the garden. "We just wanted you to know," one of the women said, "that we were very disappointed by the climate change activities today." She looked at the other two women, who nodded their agreement. "It was *very* disruptive. They were even using a *microphone*. We *came* here for the peace."

The women then walked out to their car.

This was our first Family Saturday of the year. What with the cold and the rain and the coronavirus outbreak, only a few dozen people had shown up, probably the most peaceful Saturday I'd worked at the Garden in three years. The climate change program consisted of a gentle musical performance, a bit of theater, and a few readings. The place was hardly a mosh pit.

Seattle's Japanese Garden lies beside Lake Washington Boulevard, the only thoroughfare through the Arboretum and the fastest route through this part of the city. The street is always busy during operating hours, any day of the week. The most frequent complaint we heard from visitors was about all the traffic, which produced far more noise than anything a handful of artists performing under umbrellas beside bare cherry trees could generate.

Japanese gardens typically take advantage of something called a "borrowed view." The area surrounding a garden may not officially be part of that garden, but because it can be seen from the various pathways, it becomes part of the experience. Seattle's garden, inside the 230-acre Arboretum, is surrounded by tall, lush trees and steep hills on both sides. Bald eagles and osprey sometimes fly overhead. On a good day, a blue heron might swoop down to wade in the koi pond, stalking the fish for hours. At closing time, we might see a family of raccoons making their way to the water's edge for dinner.

One famous garden in Japan is situated right next to a hospital. Part of its borrowed ambiance is the wail of emergency sirens.

The three unhappy middle-aged visitors on Family Saturday seemed to be telling me, "We *wanted* to enjoy *this* Japanese garden that's completely unaffected by climate change."

But our garden, like every other, has a "borrowed emergency," a climate crisis far more dire than the blossoming pandemic of COVID-19, as bad as that may turn out to be. During my lunch break, I caught up on the news, learning that hundreds of empty planes flew "ghost flights" over Europe because of rules which took flight slots away from airlines if their planes stayed on the ground.

My job with the Parks department requires me to walk through the entire Japanese Garden every morning before opening the gates. On a cloudy day, when I look down into the koi pond from the Moon Viewing platform, I feel I'm staring off a cliff into a bank of clouds far below. I listen to the waterfall flowing past the teahouse. I look up, beyond the borders of the garden into the Arboretum, where there are old-growth cedar, fir trees, even a few giant Sequoia.

But if you come to Seattle and stop by the Japanese Garden, don't expect it to be a refuge from the world. Even the most tranquil, apolitical spots anywhere on the face of the Earth are surrounded by climate disaster. If we want peace, and I think most of us do, we'll need to do more than complain about climate activists. We'll have to address the climate crisis itself. And it's just possible that might require us to listen to people using a microphone when reading climate poetry in the rain.

Washing Our Hands After Using the Bathroom Isn't a Sin

One of the young men in my Teachers' Quorum sometimes picked his nose before tearing apart the sacrament bread and placing pieces on several sacrament trays to be passed among the congregation. A few years later, I discovered that one of my missionary companions in Italy only bathed once a week on Preparation Day. Another took a shower every morning but never washed his hands after using the bathroom. Still another only occasionally brushed his teeth.

These behaviors might sound gross to secular ears, but they all have one thing in common—they demonstrate that Mormons have a deep, abiding faith in God. Other, less dedicated people might be forced to face the consequences of their bacterial choices, but Heavenly Father protects the worthy.

Only the faithless, many Mormons insist at rallies and city council meetings, wear masks to reduce the spread of COVID.

This pattern can be seen among other Christian evangelicals and fundamentalists as well.

While LDS Church leaders have officially encouraged members to wear masks, too many members believe such pronouncements are like the 1890 Manifesto "ordering" members to stop engaging in plural marriage. Members "knew" polygamy was still God's law and continued practicing it secretly until 1904.

Some Mormons have publicly called the First Presidency "false prophets" for endorsing mask mandates. They're upset that Church leaders seem to be bowing to pressure from the liberal media. Since the protesters don't believe in science, they can't understand the possibility that Church leaders might. Apparently not even President Russell M. Nelson, a former heart surgeon.

Mask-deniers can, of course, excuse church members in California, Oregon, Colorado, and Washington for wearing masks. Face coverings are perfectly appropriate when people are dealing with smoke from wildfires. That's just plain common sense.

But wearing a mask to reduce the spread of disease?

Apostasy. Tyranny.

Fortunately, most Mormons are smarter than that. And more faithful.

Just like my missionary companion in Rome who cooked a huge pot of spaghetti sauce one week in June and left it on top of the stove for several days, so we could enjoy homemade "sugo" the rest of the week without needing to redo the work.

When the sauce turned green on Day Three, my companion was confused. "We didn't have this problem back in Napoli," he said.

"Last winter, you mean? In that unheated apartment?"

"Yeah." He scratched his head, perplexed.

None of the missionary apartments had air conditioning, either.

I remember the day years earlier when my middle school friend, Jeff, came home with me after band practice. He soon began feeling a pain in his right side, which grew worse over the next couple of hours, especially upsetting because we couldn't reach his mom.

Fortunately, our bishop lived only a few blocks away. We called him, and while waiting for his arrival, I comforted my friend. "He holds the priesthood," I explained. Jeff was Catholic and didn't understand these things. "He'll give you a blessing and you'll be good as new."

By the time the bishop showed up, Jeff was lying on my bed, unable to do anything but moan. The bishop asked him a few questions, pressed on his lower right abdomen, and turned to the rest of us.

"No doubt about it," he said. "Appendicitis. Get this guy to a hospital."

Our bishop, I should point out, was a gastroenterologist. He's still a faithful member of the Church 45 years after this incident. Surprisingly, it turns out that faithful members aren't forbidden from accepting science as real, despite the general attitude expressed by mask deniers.

In Microbiology lab, my professor had all the students bring *E. coli* cultures from our own microbiome to class. The day we worked with *Streptococcus pyogenes*, she told us, "Last year, one of the students developed scarlet fever. Remember, guys, we're not just doing 'academic' work. These bacteria are alive."

Bacteria, mold and fungal spores, particulates in the air. Viruses. All real.

The only reason so many members of the LDS Church ignore science is that over the years, we've started putting more of our faith in the Republican Party than in our religion.

We're members now of The Church of Jesus Christ of Latter-day Republicans.

Many other American Christians seem to have made similar choices.

The good news is that we don't have to worry any longer about "evil" Democrats destroying our faith or "attacking Christianity." We've chosen to do it quite efficiently ourselves.

Triage for an Injured America

Have you ever gone to the emergency room for treatment? Been injured in a military conflict? The first step in treating the sick or wounded is triage. Which patients need help most urgently *and*, of those most seriously in need, which are most likely to benefit from immediate treatment? Americans today on both the political right and left, plus those in the center and anywhere else, can agree at least on one thing—our country is seriously injured and needs help desperately.

But *which* injuries must be attended to first? Once the most seriously compromised patient reaches the front of the line and we discover he or she presents with multiple problems, we're faced with a *second* layer of triage. Do we treat the bullet wound first or the athlete's foot? Do we treat the paper cut or the dangerously low blood glucose? The septicemia or the seasonal allergies? The Stage 2 cancer or the aneurysm?

If we start a patient on a three-week treatment plan to address their dry skin while leaving the broken leg unset, the bone will heal incorrectly and need to be broken again and reset before the patient has any chance of a full recovery. Priorities matter. Slow, incremental "progress" when a person is dying right before our eyes isn't going to get the job done.

In the middle of a pandemic which has already killed over 300,000 Americans and caused millions to lose their employer-sponsored health insurance, why is subsidizing fossil fuel corporations a priority over Medicare for All? As we triage our nation's needs, why is granting corporations immunity for exposing their employees and customers to COVID a higher priority than paying landlords not to evict tenants unemployed through no fault of their own? Or paying employees directly to stay home and reduce the spread of the virus? Why is a tax break for the wealthiest 1% more "urgent" than food for displaced workers or keeping small businesses afloat or paying restaurants to stay closed?

It's not that we don't have the resources to treat "the masses." While the limited doses of monoclonal antibodies might only be enough to treat the wealthy and politically connected, we have more than sufficient funds to cover Medicare for All and provide most everything else. We could divert a full half of our military budget to address our many other national vulnerabilities and *still* spend more on our military than any other country in the world. We could divert half of our police budgets to fund mental health agents to deal with mental health crises in a more effective manner than wielding guns and tasers, to educate and hire social workers to deal with issues even the best police officers simply aren't trained to handle.

With the stock market trading on water futures because of increasing scarcity, and the climate crisis accelerating even faster than predicted, we can triage our response by funding more drilling and pipelines *or* by developing less damaging sources of energy.

If a patient is rushed to the emergency room with a stab wound to the gut, does the doctor grab a scalpel and plunge it into the patient's neck?

So why do we choose such an insane political approach to treat the wounds of global warming and pollution and income inequality and racism?

We don't need political "saviors" determined to keep fracking wells going so that workers won't be displaced. We need our public servants to retrain workers and create environmentally sustainable jobs for us.

If a patient is diagnosed with celiac disease, do we send them back home without any instructions on how to eat so that their body can thrive?

So why don't we teach civics classes at every level? Why do we refuse to educate our citizenry by guaranteeing tuition-free college and vocational training to all? Are we satisfied when our patients are only 62% gangrene-free?

We don't recruit our medical team from applicants with no professional training. So why do we expect our untrained, uneducated citizens to be able to heal their own injuries? Or the illnesses of their neighbors? Or solve any problems at all?

One of those problems is that while some on the medical team are healers, others are serial killers disguised as angels of mercy.

How can we tell which is which? By watching how they triage patients and care.

We all see the desperate situation we're in as Americans. Some believe the solution is to kill off half the country so that there are more resources for the survivors. The rest of us realize we have more than enough resources even now, in the midst of medical and financial chaos, to treat everyone in the emergency room.

We can "save" billionaires by giving them billions of dollars more and leaving everyone else to fight over the remaining pennies.

Or we can save almost everyone, including the wealthy, by ensuring that every American has healthcare, education, housing, and a survivable climate.

We *can* save America's life, if we address the most urgent needs first.

Taking Pictures of the Tsunami

Currently out of work because of the pandemic, too afraid as cases explode across the country even to apply for other jobs, I spend a bit too much time watching YouTube videos, hoping my savings will hold out long enough for me to get the vaccine. There's one video explaining how the majority of patrons at the Beverly Hills Supper Club failed to evacuate when told the building was on fire. They didn't see any flames, didn't smell any smoke. It couldn't be that serious.

Is that what *we're* doing as we laugh at Sidney Powell and Rudy Giuliani?

Another video I watched showed campers in Los Alfaques encountering an unexpected fog that was clearly no cause for alarm, unaware that more than 200 of them would soon be dead. The most incredible part of watching disasters unfold is seeing people about to meet their doom go on about their lives, oblivious despite all the warnings.

The day after Christmas, a family at a seaside resort in Thailand films approaching waves from their deck, laughing as they see boats overturned and people on the beach suddenly in knee-deep water. The vacationing family continues filming as the next wave crashes into the beach, the water now almost to the top of the wall separating their hotel property from the ocean.

They keep filming as the next, higher wave comes barreling toward the shore. Suddenly, they start screaming and running as the water crashes against them.

What the hell were they thinking?

In Japan, someone films a tsunami flowing upriver. The videographer is filming from a balcony three stories up. We see the concrete wall separating the river from the town. Two folks on bicycles casually pedal downriver, *toward the coast*, while we watch large boats on the other side of the wall being tossed about, crashing into bridges, being ripped apart and sinking. We watch as the river rises and rises until it overtops the wall. Black water comes crashing into the town, carrying fishing boats and other debris. Cars are soon added to the flow.

Where are the two casual bicyclists?

It's easy in hindsight to ridicule the foolishness in gathering along the beach to watch an approaching tsunami. What idiots.

I wonder what people will say about us ten or fifteen years from now. "Didn't they see what was about to happen? Wasn't it obvious?"

Will they be asking these questions about a coup and overthrow of the election? Will they be asking about widespread white supremacist terrorism?

Will folks be asking because we thought "just this once," we could take our masks off to have dinner with a friend?

Will the questions be posed because the Democratic Party has self-destructed by refusing to embrace the working class and offering more than lip service to Blacks, Latinx, and other historically and currently oppressed groups?

Maybe they'll be asking these questions because we still refused, in the face of overwhelming evidence, to address the climate emergency.

I listen to pundits on TV insisting "the guardrails are holding" against the multiple coup attempts we've already witnessed, and I think of the two bicyclists killed while pedaling along the river. The concrete barriers did hold, even under the weight of all that water.

But "holding" isn't enough when a tsunami is coming.

We need to build higher, stronger walls, as the mayor of Fudai did, his coastal village surviving the 2011 Japanese tsunami almost unscathed.

It means we don't "forgive and forget" the crimes committed against democracy.

It means we pay people to stay home until the pandemic is under control.

It means we ban all new fossil fuel extraction and pipelines.

It means we cancel all student loan debt, one of the simplest ways to start the long process of reparations.

It means we implement universal healthcare so that our citizens are no longer crushed under pharmaceutical overlords.

It means much more even than this. But the one thing it *doesn't* mean is that we relax and go on about our lives as if nothing important is happening just one hundred yards away.

We can survive a tsunami, but only if we take immediate action.

My HIV Infection Taught Me to Treat Everyone as if They're Contagious

As I self-isolate at home, I see folks a block down from me hosting birthday parties. I see friends of mine getting together for various other reasons, some trying to keep a safe physical distance but others in the same group offering comforting back rubs during this stressful period. These folks want to show that they aren't afraid of their friends. They don't want to insult family members. But acting sensibly doesn't mean panicking and accusing everyone of trying to kill you. As a gay man who came out in the 1980s, I understand that the only reasonable course of action at a time like this is to assume *everyone* is infected.

By the time I came out, the AIDS pandemic was well underway. I first learned of the disease from a one-paragraph article on the back page of my hometown newspaper in late 1982. I understood the impact immediately and wondered why that information wasn't on the front page. But I knew the answer, even as a virginal, former Mormon missionary: the disease was affecting people who didn't matter, and bigotry was preventing the populace as a whole from realizing they weren't immune.

COVID-19 has become politicized as well. Perhaps it happens with every major disease. In the Middle Ages, bubonic plague was often blamed on the Jews. Hundreds of years later, Germans blamed the French for syphilis. In 19th-century America, the Irish were blamed for cholera outbreaks. The blaming only hurt communities. It never helped.

I didn't start dating men until 1987, so I *never* had unsafe sex. It was clear that the only sensible way to interact sexually with other men was to assume they were all HIV+. Perhaps they hadn't been tested and didn't know their status. Perhaps they'd been infected since their last test. Perhaps they were lying, afraid no one would have sex with them if they told the truth. It didn't really matter. The bottom line was that the only reasonable course of action was to assume *everyone* had the virus and behave accordingly.

I admit, I had a lot of sex. Some of the other guys were negative, but a good many of them were positive. I wasn't afraid of men with HIV. I simply took precautions. There was no need to make anyone an outcast.

Even one of my long-term partners had HIV, but I never caught the virus from him. We simply made efforts to be careful.

After we broke up, though, and I was playing with others again, I made a single mistake. One. *One* mistake. Playing with two elderly neighbors, I was surprised when one of the men penetrated me without first putting on a condom.

That wasn't cool, I thought. But I didn't want to offend the guy. So I didn't insist he back out. At least for the next ten seconds. Then I repositioned myself so that my desired goal was achieved without having to say anything. That way, I didn't have to take part in an awkward conversation that might hurt his feelings.

But ten seconds was all it took. Just one encounter with an infected man during which I behaved in a foolish manner radically changed the rest of my life.

Several days later, I became ill and passed out while waiting for the health clinic to open. Even so, I thought all I had was strep throat. I'd already forgotten about those ten foolhardy seconds. So a couple of months later, when a local hospital began accepting applicants for an HIV vaccine trial, I went in to be tested. I assumed I'd still be negative, as I had been after every other test, and would therefore qualify.

I didn't qualify.

While some of my Mormon relatives believed I contracted HIV because I was a terrible sinner, the truth is I was infected because I was careless.

We can't be foolish and worry about offending our friends and family by assuming they are infected with the coronavirus. It doesn't mean we're accusing them of anything. It's not a slap in the face. It doesn't mean we think they're morally deficient in any way.

The corollary is for *us* not to feel offended when our friends and loved ones assume *we're* infected and act accordingly.

My husband and I have been together over 12 years. We only have safe sex. I am not offended because we take precautions. I'm happy that he is still HIV negative.

Many of us are going to develop COVID-19. It's far more communicable than HIV. But we can flatten the curve and make survival possible for more patients and healthcare workers if we just accept the new normal. *Immediately.*

We don't need to panic. We just need to be careful around everyone, including—no, especially—the ones we love.

Which Scrooge Are You?

At the beginning of Charles Dickens's *A Christmas Carol*, when Ebenezer Scrooge contemplates the death of his employee's ill child and many others like him, he says dismissively, "If they would rather die, they had better do it, and decrease the surplus population." Scrooge, of course, is concerned only about making money, whatever the consequences to others. He begrudges Bob Cratchit enough coal to heat his office. He complains about giving his clerk a day off to celebrate the birth of Jesus with his family. He suggests that the poor might be better off in prison.

Here at the start of the COVID-19 pandemic, we're already hearing corporate and political leaders insisting we open businesses again as soon as possible, often weeks or even months before health officials deem it safe. Some governors don't even want to close down in the first place. "The cure" will be worse than the pandemic, they claim. Think of the people who will die because they've lost their jobs, become homeless, become depressed and suicidal over their financial circumstances. Business leaders whose actions never took into account the sufferings of the poor before insist they are now doing folks a *favor* by forcing them back to work. Several prominent older folks with plenty of insurance and money to stay holed up for months nobly and publicly pretend they're willing to give up their own lives "for the country."

Of course, gold promoters like Glenn Beck and conservative politicians like Dan Patrick won't be the ones dying. It will be the poor or nearly poor who have no choice but to risk infection every day at work who will do most of the dying.

Along with a good many middle-class folks who adhere to various iterations of the prosperity gospel, afraid that a temporary reduction in funds will indicate a loss of favor with their God.

Voluntary as well as conscripted risk takers all working together to decrease the surplus population.

The White House has no problem throwing trillions of dollars at Wall Street for the good of the country. But suspending (not postponing) rent payments for residents? And lease payments for small businesses? Absolving student loan debt? Tying the trillions bestowed upon corporations to mandatory paychecks for employees? The only reason anyone would lose their job, become homeless, or become depressed or suicidal over their financial situation is if we insist on making sure their financial situation remains dire.

That's a choice, not a natural consequence of pandemics. Other countries, like Denmark and Belgium and the Netherlands, have made a different choice, one that prioritizes people over profits. Or at least puts them *somewhere* on the list of priorities.

At some point, people will obviously need to go back to work. Society can't function indefinitely without labor. But a few weeks into a war against a deadly pathogen is hardly the time for capitulation. Friends of mine, even some colleagues from my Mormon missionary days, talk about the need to sacrifice those most vulnerable for the sake of "the country." Those with chronic health problems are unhappy in the best of times. The elderly have already had their chance at life. They'll only be around a few more years anyway. Why should the rest of us suffer because grandma wants to play with her grandchildren? She can see them just fine from heaven.

While people of any age can become seriously ill or die from COVID-19, the death rate starts rising sharply for people 60 and over. I realize many Americans lack proficiency in math, but do we need a scientist to point out that a 60-year-old could easily live another 30 years? The "elderly" are not at death's door and simply being pushed through a few days early. Even a 70-year-old with diabetes could have several good years left. Mary Tyler Moore lived to be 80. Do we really want to tell folks like Laura Petrie and Mary Richards, "We liked you in your prime, but we have no further use for you, so goodbye and good luck"?

My conservative and religious friends often claim that all abortion is murder. *They* value the sanctity of life. Apparently, though, life loses its divine stamp of approval if it interferes with corporate profits. Children get little societal assistance once they're out of the womb. Even in the midst of massive layoffs, with people around the world dying from the coronavirus by the thousands, my conservative family can't accept that tying health insurance to the workplace is a fundamentally flawed policy.

Fortunately, health officials have insisted that we not send people back to non-essential jobs to infect each other just yet. So for now, we can still sit at home and read a good book. Maybe something inspirational from Dickens. Ebenezer Scrooge did, after all, learn to value life in the end. And an early novel by the author of *Robinson Crusoe*, who clearly understood something about social distancing, might be enlightening as well. Perhaps his *Journal of the Plague Year*.

If we want to do something as a family, though, something *fun*, we can always watch a comedy together. *Throw Momma from the Train* is trending heavily right now.

COVID Blankets for Poor People

Most of us were never taught in school that European immigrants—priests and preachers and other generous donors—often gave blankets to Native American communities to promote peace and goodwill. Blankets that sometimes were intentionally infected with smallpox. If God chose to kill off hundreds of thousands, even millions, of "savages," those sinners had no one to blame but themselves. Yet even if many Christians today were never taught this well-documented history, they seem to understand the process instinctively. They refuse to release approved funding to Native American communities dealing with the coronavirus. They supply them with malfunctioning equipment or items they haven't requested instead of the supplies they need. Some people even point their fingers and say, "If you don't like it here, go back to your own country." While specifics of our long tradition of hatred may not be widely taught, hate itself is taught in America every day—by the most righteous among us.

We teach in school and at church and in the media that we can't provide universal healthcare to our citizens because doing so would be immoral. We've provided people with decent jobs so they can pay for their own healthcare. If those jobs are in crowded meat processing plants where they must work next to hundreds of coworkers infected with COVID, that's hardly our fault.

God clearly established capitalism in the New Testament as the only humane way to run a society. Jesus spoke of it frequently, as did John the Beloved. It was Judas who spoke all the time about socialism. We bear no responsibility for handing out disease-infected jobs to the poor.

It's not like we *hate* the lazy and weak. Every day on TV, we announce our gratitude for grocery store cashiers, for Amazon warehouse workers, for bus drivers, for certified nursing assistants. They're our heroes. We do flyovers to thank them. It's not *our* fault if their employers don't make their workplaces safer. Just because we wash our hands of the problem and don't demand safety measures.

Besides, this "pandemic" is way overblown. It's clearly a plot to make Trump look bad. We all know that Democrats are part of the Deep State. Nancy Pelosi waving a flag looks like a vampire holding a cross. AOC goes to fancy hair salons. These people control the lamestream media that keep telling lies. Yes, some old, decrepit patients are dying a few weeks early, but Democrats are using inflated death tolls to hurt the middle class. The fact that tens of thousands of people are dying in other countries around the world, even in places like Brazil and Russia that are controlled by strong leaders, just shows the depths to which Democrats will go to hurt America.

Atheists are *praying* for people to die.

Of course, it's all China's fault.

Though the disease isn't very serious.

But those people eat *bats*. And chickens. And dogs.

They eat dogs in Vietnam, too, and South Korea. And in Switzerland. The Swiss even eat cats.

Asians are so disgusting.

Trump is the greatest president we've ever had. It's not *his* fault he threw out the National Security Council's pandemic response handbook that had been written during Obama's presidency. Barack *Hussein* wasn't even American, not even Christian. It's not Trump's fault he was forced to fire scientists and appoint political friends to lead the agencies we need during a pandemic. Scientists are godless. The whole reason we're being punished with all this suffering and death in the first place is because so many liberals have turned away from God.

Not that there's much death and misery actually going around. No more than usual with the seasonal flu. That can be cured pretty easily with Jim Bakker's silver solution or by injecting ourselves with UV light. If worse comes to worst, we can always let Kenneth Copeland blow on us.

It's all Hillary's fault, anyway. She should be in prison.

And everyone knows this fake "crisis" was the idea of a commie Jew to prevent Donald Trump from holding rallies. He's in cahoots with Pocahontas. Bill Gates just wants to implant chips in everyone to track us. That's why we need the government to monitor everybody's emails.

Because Big Government must be brought to its knees. And *we* should be the ones to do it, not China or Canada or Germany, because no one understands that our political system is the absolute best in the world more than we do.

"COVID-19 or COVID-1984!"

"Scamdemic!"

"Give me liberty or give me COVID-19!"

"Let my people golf!"

Even though we try hard to be loving, caring Christians, when we see reporters covering our protests—protests we're *entitled* to because of the First Amendment—we can't help but yell and curse them when they arrive wearing masks. How disrespectful! Trump should just shut down all those lefty organizations that keep spreading so much fake news. It's *their* fault there's such division in our society. We're patriots when we rip masks off stupid people or push them into ponds or cough on them or wipe our noses on their sleeves. We're really justified in doing pretty much anything we want because these infidels are deliberately hurting America. They're traitors who must pay for their treason.

Why else would we bring Confederate flags to our rallies?

"If ballots don't free us, bullets will!"

"No Room for Fascists!"

It's intellectually dishonest for Democrats to suggest the swastikas on our signs represent *us*. When we wear KKK hoods at a rally, we're making a point about *you*.

Democrats are making the virus *political*. Just when we thought they couldn't get any more despicable, they use photos of mass graves to try to manipulate people.

Thank God those are just bodies of dead crisis actors.

So we'd better go out and buy some more guns. We may have to eat our neighbors.

The Constitution gives us the right to go into any store we want without a mask. The same way business owners have every right to put up signs declaring "No Shirt, No Shoes, No Service." The same way bakers can turn away degenerate gays. If perverts want to buy a wedding cake, they have the right to go somewhere else. *We* believe in freedom of religion. People *we* refuse to serve have the God-given right to leave us alone.

But we demand the same freedom in return. By definition, Christians can't discriminate. Yet those corrupt Democratic governors won't even let us go to church. That alone proves they're secretly Satan worshippers, which we've suspected all along. We should be able to gather with all our loved ones, sit next to each other for hours singing and praising God, which we can't possibly be expected to do at home as a family. We should be able to go to work without masks, fire our employees who arrive wearing the offensive things, turn away customers who try to come into our businesses wearing such infernal objects.

It's a plot to let black people rob our stores, a plot to make everyone wear burqas. As law-abiding citizens, we should be able to go into any workplace or business we want without wearing masks.

Everyone's trying to make us follow goddamn rules all the time! We're supposed to be "PC" and not kill anyone. We simply won't have it!

We'll make the rules.

And those rules are that Trump is always right. Democrats are always wrong. Scientists and doctors are *usually* wrong, unless they agree with Trump. This isn't rocket science, after all. Above all else, we must preserve Wall Street because without it, we'll never be able to enter heaven when we die. If some poor people die, or ignorant workers, or Native American heathens, who are we to tell God how to do his job?

We're Christians. We put God first. He took this land from Tonto and gave it to *us* because we deserve it. We must do everything we can to avoid worshipping the anti-Christ. No mark of the Beast on *our* foreheads. That's why we proudly wear our red baseball caps made in China proclaiming "Make America Great Again."

It's sad, isn't it? Truly, genuinely sad, that everyone else is so terribly deluded. But we're not spiteful. All that we do is guided by love. So we are more than happy, always, to send everyone heading to the mortuary our sincerest thoughts and prayers.

Securing the Well-Being of Citizens is Not Tyranny

A former missionary colleague of mine explained that he believes both those on the right and the left want basically the same thing—to help people—but his beef is that those on the left want to achieve it through tyranny. If "the government" assists the poor, the rest of us are forced to pay higher taxes. Helping is only appropriate if the behavior is performed without coercion. It was "Satan's plan" to *make* people be good. God instead chose to give us free will. But everyone, both on the right and the left, should *want* the state to improve the lives of all its citizens.

During the current pandemic, many insist that requiring people to wear masks is heavy-handed government interference. And yet some Republican business owners deny their employees a choice by firing them if they wear a mask to work. It's economic tyranny if "big government" orders businesses to close temporarily to avoid spreading the virus, but it's not a problem if Republicans order them to reopen and immediately rescind unemployment assistance to workers who must now choose between homelessness and serious illness. A "stay at home" order to protect the public during a crisis is a violation of the First Amendment, but routinely monitoring emails and phone calls without a warrant under normal circumstances is "for the greater good" and so doesn't violate the Fourth Amendment.

Republicans claim that using tax dollars to provide everyone a college education is tyranny. But requiring every pacifist to financially support the military is no more than "responsibility." Demanding we share the burden of providing healthcare to all is a prescription for losing our souls. But compelling everyone to gift fossil fuel corporations with billions in subsidies is a divine cure for the economy. It's a sin to use a single penny of taxpayer money on abortion but it's "free will" to force women to bear the children of rapists.

My missionary colleague and I spent two years of our lives volunteering to teach others about Mormonism. But even among Mormons, free will isn't entirely free. No one is *forced* to pay ten percent of their income to the Church, but if they don't, they can't marry in the temple. They can't attend their children's weddings. They can't enter the Celestial Kingdom after they die. Our culture determines the "natural" consequences to every free choice, in order to elicit the behavior we want.

To quote Dana Carvey's Church Lady, "Isn't that conveeeenient?"

As citizens of a civilized nation, we make a social contract. If it's not tyranny to use taxpayer money to hire police officers and firefighters to protect the community, it's not tyranny to use taxes to hire doctors and nurses to protect patients. If it's not tyranny to use tax dollars to teach a child to read, it's not tyranny to provide an adult adequate job training.

Many on the right firmly believe in enforcing the policies that complement their religious or political agenda. They only protest—carrying assault weapons into state capitols as a show of "force"—if those policies make compulsory helping people they feel no compulsion to help. Grandma might die? She's so old she'd be dead in a couple of weeks, anyway. And it's not like we're condemning her to hell. She'll go straight to Paradise. Desperate asylum seekers might die in detention camps? Well, we can't help *everyone*. The truly empathetic would understand that those folks are better off in Spirit Prison where they'll finally be open to accepting the gospel.

Working together to improve the lives of all members of our society is not tyranny. It's our civic duty. It may well be the purpose of religion to help perfect our souls, but the job of the state is to secure the physical well-being of its citizens. If those on the right feel that obligating them to treat others humanely is a sin, the rest of us are free not to accept their conclusion.

But those of you on the right needn't worry. Rest assured that if you're forced against your will to protect workers, or give the unemployed an education that allows them to support their families, or stop corporations from polluting the environment, God can always punish us later for helping you.

Consistent Messaging in an Emergency

The oxygen masks drop down from above our seats. I hadn't paid attention during the pre-flight emergency spiel. I'd heard it all a thousand times before, and the flight attendants weren't singing or dancing to keep it interesting. A couple of hours after take-off, I'd looked up from the book in my lap to clear my head. *Guns, Germs, and Steel* wasn't light reading. And I'd seen two attendants whispering worriedly to each other, one of them pointing at a window or something near it. I couldn't see anything suspicious and went back to my reading as one of them picked up a handset and whispered into it.

A minute or two later, the loudspeaker crackled and the captain began speaking. "The Fasten Seatbelt sign is on. We may run into some minor turbulence, but don't be alarmed."

And that was that. The flight attendants smiled cheerily, if a bit plastically, and encouraged a few passengers to buckle up. I felt a little unnerved when one of the attendants closed his eyes and mouthed something to himself, but then he smiled again, and I went back to my reading.

And then the masks fell. Passengers are shouting out questions now as the tubes dangle before us. An elderly couple two rows ahead scream in terror, immature old people. One of the flight attendants grabs her headset and orders the adults in the cabin to put on oxygen masks before helping our children. "Or you may pass out before you can help your child."

"Oh my god!" someone else screams. I'm already tired of the melodrama.

Just as I begin pulling the elastic bands behind my head, the captain comes over the loudspeaker again. "Please stay calm. The oxygen masks deployed accidentally. We are in no danger. If you feel any shortness of breath, it's because you're overexcited. Calm down and breathe normally."

I can hear nervous laughter from the passengers near me, mixed with angry accusations. One middle-aged man across the aisle punches in a nasty text to the airline. A young woman kisses her daughter's hair ribbon, telling the girl not to worry. My heart is beating so fast it hurts. My son starts crying because I'm squeezing his hand too tightly.

Looking out the window, I see that we're descending slowly. We're going to be OK.

The "Fasten Seatbelt" sign goes off. An elderly man stands and heads for the bathroom. Who knew there were so many old people?

"Please take your seat immediately!" a flight attendant yells at him.

"But—"

"There's a crack in the window!" the flight attendant screams. She's quite unprofessional.

Obviously, if there were really a problem with the oxygen level, we'd all be unconscious by now, so the emergency must be overblown. Surely, the captain knows more than these flight attendants, who are really no more than glorified waiters and waitresses. Why would a crack cause all the masks to fall? Someone just pushed an emergency button when they didn't need to. A passenger might have had a heart attack because of this reckless behavior. I'm appalled. I pull out my phone to send a stern text to the airline as well.

But my phone is ripped out of my hand when the cabin experiences explosive decompression. The elderly man flies down the aisle along with the flight attendant yelling at him. Books and laptops zip past, hitting passengers on the head, tearing off a piece of someone's forehead here, a tuft of hair there.

I grab my oxygen mask, fumbling for it in the wind and panic, barely managing to cover my face before I see my son slumped over in his seat. My heart pounding harder than ever, I slip his mask on, and after what seems an eternity, he slowly begins to stir.

There's no point dragging the analogy out any further, especially since no analogy is perfect. But the one thing anyone trained to handle an emergency knows is that consistent messaging is important. Even as a cashier, I'm trained by my employer in First Aid and CPR. One of the first steps is to take control of the situation. We don't look around timidly and say, "Anyone want to call 9-1-1?" We point to someone and order them. "YOU, call 9-1-1! And YOU, wait by the curb to wave the medics down."

If it turns out that in an actual emergency, we're too emotionally shaken to perform as we've been trained, we can practice later to be more prepared the next time. But if after three months of daily practice, we still can't make it through an announcement without changing our mind in mid-sentence, or becoming so flustered we simply turn around and walk off, I think it's clear this is not something we're ever going to be good at. It doesn't mean we're not great at a hundred other things, but leading in an emergency is obviously not one of them.

Even if we're generally inclined to trust captains over flight attendants, I hope we can all agree that at the very least, we need a new captain, one who doesn't deny the reality of what's happening aboard the plane he's piloting. Assuming we survive the current catastrophe, we can stick with the same airline next time or move to one of several competitors, but for God's sake, let's choose a captain who isn't going to kill us.

Conclusion

Keeping the Pantry Full: Freedom and Justice Demand Constant Vigilance

"I can't wait till the Mueller report comes out." "I can't wait until the mid-term elections." "I can't wait till we elect a new president in 2020." "We'll never achieve equality until we abandon capitalism and adopt socialism." Almost everyone I know is working hard to get us out of the terrible political predicament we're currently in, but only a handful seem to recognize that none of these things is a permanent fix. Justice, freedom, and equality don't have fairy tale endings. There's no moment after which we can live happily ever after. Maintaining freedom and justice and equality will be a constant battle, not only in our lifetimes but forever.

Have we ever heard someone say, "I finally got all the weeds out of my yard. I never have to worry about that nasty task again"?

Have we heard anyone say, "Whew. I'm finally down to my ideal weight and BMI. Now I can stop exercising and watching what I eat"?

Or "I finally have the right to marry, and I've married the man of my dreams. It's all coasting from here"?

Whatever our personal end goals are for "progress," whether that be electing anyone other than Trump, or trying to get Democrats to move to the left, or to implement full-fledged socialism, Election Day is not the end of the struggle. The "Revolution" is not the end.

The work we do is hard. We want it to be over. We want to "win" and finally have a chance to breathe, but the painful truth is we can never relax.

Critics of reform point out that reforms can always be undone. That's true. But revolution and complete overhaul can be undone, too. The people's revolution in Russia didn't bring about lasting change. Within a decade, socialism had been corrupted into communism. Before long, Russia and then the Soviet Union were oppressive tyrannies. After "the revolution" in Cuba, its citizens still faced a dictatorship that threw LGBTQ folks and dissenters into prison.

Everything can be undone. That doesn't mean we shouldn't push Dems to the left, that we shouldn't try to shift to Democratic Socialism, that we shouldn't bring about Trotsky socialism. It just means that whatever path we choose, we must realize our end goals are no more secure than anyone else's. Your system may very well be better than my system, but it's every bit as susceptible to failure as any other.

That's because human beings will be implementing and sustaining each and every type of system we ever develop, and no humans of any persuasion are perfect. It seems a trite and obvious point, but every day I see people who think that if they get *their* way, if *their* idea of the perfect candidate or perfect policy or perfect economic or political system is victorious, we'll finally be OK.

We can be better, but we'll never be OK.

That doesn't mean we fall into cynicism or despair. We just need realistic expectations.

Protecting and preserving something great is a never-ending battle. Religious fanatics in the past decade have destroyed Persian artifacts dating back nearly 2000 years. Catholic invaders 500 years ago destroyed every Mayan book they could find. Thousands of temples, churches, synagogues, and mosques around the world, some of them hundreds of years old, have been destroyed over the years by enemies of the worshippers who met there.

We can preserve national parks against predators (you know, coal and oil companies, loggers, off-road recreational vehicles) every day for decades and decades, but all that work can be undone overnight once one of those predators finally gets in. It's far easier to cut down a 2000-year-old tree than it is to protect it every day against every possible threat.

Holocaust survivors are murdered 70 years after their liberation from the camps. We can clean up Superfund sites, and they can be polluted once again. We can develop antibiotics, and bacteria can evolve to withstand them.

Our work demanding justice and equality doesn't have an end date. There will *never* be a time when we can let our guard down.

This necessity for constant vigilance is true in every other part of our lives. Why in the world would we expect something different in the political and economic world? Because *those* things are simpler, smaller, and easier to control?

We must fight to make the world a better place, but we must do so with the understanding that such an endeavor requires a permanent commitment. Every advance we achieve must be supervised and monitored. We must always maintain oversight. We must continually keep pressure on all involved to preserve each and every victory.

Part of that is recruiting and training the next generation, and the one after that, to take over the fight when we're too old and tired to keep going. Another part is to let them come up with ideas and plans of their own. We can tag team with others so we can take a temporary break in the battle when we're weary.

It helps to remember that past leaders may have been tremendous heroes but that doesn't make every word they wrote scripture. If bacteria can adapt to new conditions, we can, too.

We just returned from the dentist with clean teeth and a clean bill of health, with no cavities or gum disease? That's great, but we'd better keep brushing and flossing. If a new prophylactic treatment becomes available, we'd be wise to include it.

Folks in AA take things "one day at a time." They understand a universal truth, that one must always maintain constant vigilance, that even thirty or forty years of sobriety can be lost with a single night of drinking.

I understand those on the left who find both Biden and Harris too weak on too many issues to support their candidacy, but if we're going to cast a protest vote, let's protest the clear and present danger in the White House now.

When my doctor told me I had to do three or more daily finger sticks to monitor my diabetes, I insisted on using a 14-day continuous glucose monitoring device instead. "It's not as good," he insisted. "You need instant results."

"Doctor," I replied, "you're going to need to deal with the patient you have, not the one you wish you had."

When I recounted the story to my husband, he said, "That's the way we handle our marriage, isn't it? We deal with the partner we have, not the one we wish we had."

It sounds offensive, but the reality is no patient is perfect, no spouse is perfect. If we refuse to treat patients until they're perfect, a lot of sick folks are going to die. If we will only marry and stay married to perfect spouses, we're going to be alone a very long time.

Likewise, we need to deal with the political system we have, not the one we wish we had. We can certainly work to improve the system or change it altogether but abstaining from participation in the meantime when so much is at stake is itself complicit behavior.

Once we get the exact candidate we want, though, once we establish the reforms, laws, and economic systems we want, we can still never let our guard down.

We just got back from the grocery and filled our fridge? Would any of us ever consider that a *final* victory?

In any event, I've said my piece. Everything should be fine now. And it's time for some happily ever after semi-annual maintenance sex with my husband. He seems reluctant to head into the bedroom with me, but I really don't understand why. I bathed last month, didn't I? I'm good.

Books by Johnny Townsend

Thanks for reading! If you enjoyed this book, could you please take a few minutes to write a review online? Reviews are helpful both to me as an author and to other readers, so we'd all sincerely appreciate your writing one! And if you did enjoy the book, here are some others I've written you might want to look up:

Mormon Underwear

God's Gargoyles

The Circumcision of God

Sex among the Saints

Dinosaur Perversions

Zombies for Jesus

The Abominable Gayman

The Gay Mormon Quilter's Club

The Golem of Rabbi Loew

Mormon Fairy Tales

Flying over Babel

Marginal Mormons

Mormon Bullies

The Mormon Victorian Society

Dragons of the Book of Mormon

Selling the City of Enoch

A Day at the Temple

Behind the Zion Curtain

Gayrabian Nights

Lying for the Lord

Despots of Deseret

Missionaries Make the Best Companions

Invasion of the Spirit Snatchers

The Tyranny of Silence

Sex on the Sabbath

The Washing of Brains

The Mormon Inquisition

Interview with a Mission President

Weeping, Wailing, and Gnashing of Teeth

Behind the Bishop's Door

The Moat around Zion

The Last Days Linger

Mormon Madness

Human Compassion for Beginners

Dead Mankind Walking

Who Invited You to the Orgy?

Breaking the Promise of the Promised Land

I Will, Through the Veil

Am I My Planet's Keeper?

Have Your Cum and Eat It, Too

Strangers with Benefits

What Would Anne Frank Do?

This Is All Just Too Hard

Glory to the Glory Hole!

My Pre-Bucket List

Blessed Are the Firefighters

Wake Up and Smell the Missionaries

Quilting Beyond the Rainbow

Gay Sleeping Arrangements

Queer Quilting

Racism by Proxy

Orgy at the STD Clinic

Life Is Better with Love

Please Evacuate

Recommended Daily Humanity

The Camper Killings

Let the Faggots Burn: The UpStairs Lounge Fire

Latter-Gay Saints: An Anthology of Gay Mormon Fiction (co-editor)

Available from your favorite online or neighborhood bookstore.

Wondering what some of those other books are about? Read on!

Invasion of the Spirit Snatchers

During the Apocalypse, a group of Mormon survivors in Hurricane, Utah gather in the home of the Relief Society president, telling stories to pass the time as they ration their food storage and await the Second Coming. But this is no ordinary group of Mormons— or perhaps it is. They are the faithful, feminist, gay, apostate, and repentant, all working together to help each other through the darkest days any of them have yet seen.

Gayrabian Nights

Gayrabian Nights is a twist on the well-known classic, *1001 Arabian Nights*, in which Scheherazade, under the threat of death if she ceases to captivate King Shahryar's attention, enchants him through a series of mysterious, adventurous, and romantic tales.

In this variation, a male escort, invited to the hotel room of a closeted, homophobic Mormon senator, learns that the man is poised to vote on a piece of anti-gay legislation the following morning. To prevent him from sleeping, so that the exhausted senator will miss casting his vote on the Senate floor, the escort entertains him with stories of homophobia, celibacy, mixed orientation marriages, reparative therapy, coming out, first love, gay marriage, and long-term successful gay relationships. The escort crafts the stories to give the senator a crash course in gay culture and sensibilities, hoping to bring the man closer to accepting his own sexual orientation.

Let the Faggots Burn: The UpStairs Lounge Fire

On Gay Pride Day in 1973, someone set the entrance to a French Quarter gay bar on fire. In the terrible inferno that followed, thirty-two people lost their lives, including a third of the local congregation of the Metropolitan Community Church, their pastor burning to death halfway out a second-story window as he tried to claw his way to freedom. A mother who'd gone to the bar with her two gay sons died alongside them. A man who'd helped his friend escape first was found dead near the fire escape. Two children waited outside a movie theater across town for a father and step-father who would never pick them up. During this era of rampant homophobia, several families refused to claim the bodies, and many churches refused to bury the dead. Author Johnny Townsend pored through old records and tracked down survivors of the fire as well as relatives and friends of those killed to compile this fascinating account of a forgotten moment in gay history.

The Abominable Gayman

What is a gay Mormon missionary doing in Italy? He is trying to save his own soul as well as the souls of others. In these tales chronicling the two-year mission of Robert Anderson, we see a young man tormented by his inability to be the man the Church says he should be. In addition to his personal hell, Anderson faces a major earthquake, organized crime, a serious bus accident, and much more. He copes with horrendous mission leaders and his own suicidal tendencies. But one day, he meets another missionary who loves him, and his world changes forever.

Missionaries Make the Best Companions

What lies behind the freshly scrubbed façades of the Mormon missionaries we see about town? In these stories, an ex-Mormon tries to seduce a faithful elder by showing him increasingly suggestive movies. A sister missionary fulfills her community service requirement by babysitting for a prostitute. Two elders break their mission rules by venturing into the forbidden French Quarter. A senior missionary couple try to reactivate lapsed members while their own family falls apart back home. A young man hopes that serving a second full-time mission will lead him up the Church hierarchy. Two bored missionaries decide to make a little extra money moonlighting in a male stripper club. Two frustrated elders find an acceptable way to masturbate—by donating to a Fertility Clinic. A lonely man searches for the favorite companion he hasn't seen in thirty years.

The Golem of Rabbi Loew

Jacob and Esau Cohen are the closest of brothers. In fact, they're lovers. A doctor tries to combine canine genes with those of Jews, to improve their chances of surviving a hostile world. A Talmudic scholar dates an escort. A scientist tries to develop the "God spot" in the brains of his patients in order to create a messiah. The Golem of Prague is really Rabbi Loew's secret lover. While some of the Jews in Townsend's book are Orthodox, this collection of Jewish stories most certainly is not.

The Last Days Linger

The scriptures tell us that in the Last Days, wickedness will increase upon the Earth. When leaders of the Mormon Church see a rise in the number of gay members, they believe the end is upon them. But while "wickedness never was happiness," it begins to appear that wickedness can sometimes be divine. At least, the stories here suggest that religious proscriptions condemning homosexuality have it all wrong. While gay Mormons may be no closer to perfection than anyone else, they're no further from it, either. And sometimes, being gay provides just the right ingredient to create saints—as flawed as God himself.

Mormon Madness

Mental illness can strike the faithful as easily as anyone else. But often religious doctrine and practice exacerbate rather than alleviate these problems. From schizophrenia to obsessive-compulsive disorder, from persecution complex to sexual dysfunction, autism to dissociative identity disorder, Mormons must cope with their mental as well as their spiritual health on a daily basis.

Am I My Planet's Keeper?

Global Warming. Climate Change. Climate Crisis. Climate Emergency. Whatever label we use, we are facing one of the greatest challenges to the survival of life as we know it.

But while addressing greenhouse gases is perhaps our most urgent need, it's not our only task. We must also address toxic waste, pollution, habitat destruction, and our other contributions to the world's sixth mass extinction event.

In order to do that, we must simultaneously address the unmet human needs that keep us distracted from deeper engagement in stabilizing our climate: moderating economic inequality, guaranteeing healthcare to all, and ensuring education for everyone.

And to accomplish *that*, we must unite to combat the monied forces that use fear, prejudice, and misinformation to manipulate us.

It's a daunting task. But success is our only option.

Wake Up and Smell the Missionaries

Two Mormon missionaries in Italy discover they share the same rare ability—both can emit pheromones on demand. At first, they playfully compete in the hills of Frascati to see who can tempt "investigators" most. But soon they're targeting each other non-stop.

Can two immature young men learn to control their "superpower" to live a normal life…and develop genuine love? Even as their relationship is threatened by the attentions of another man?

They seem just on the verge of success when a massive earthquake leaves them trapped under the rubble of their apartment in Castellammare.

With night falling and temperatures dropping, can they dig themselves out in time to save themselves? And will their injuries destroy the ability that brought them together in the first place?

Orgy at the STD Clinic

Todd Tillotson is struggling to move on after his husband is killed in a hit and run attack a year earlier during a Black Lives Matter protest in Seattle.

In this novel set entirely on public transportation, we watch as Todd, isolated throughout the pandemic, battles desperation in his attempt to safely reconnect with the world.

Will he find love again, even casual friendship, or will he simply end up another crazy old man on the bus?

Things don't look good until a man whose face he can't even see sits down beside him despite the raging variants.

And asks him a question that will change his life.

Please Evacuate

A gay, partygoing New Yorker unconcerned about the future or the unsustainability of capitalism is hit by a truck and thrust into a straight man's body half a continent away. As Hunter tries to figure out what's happening, he's caught up in another disaster, a wildfire sweeping through a Colorado community, the flames overtaking him and several schoolchildren as they flee.

When he awakens, Hunter finds himself in the body of yet another man, this time in northern Italy, a former missionary about to marry a young Mormon woman. Still piecing together this new reality, and beginning to embrace his latest identity, Hunter fights for his life in a devastating flash flood along with his wife *and* his new husband.

He's an aging worker in drought-stricken Texas, a nurse at an assisted living facility in the direct path of a hurricane, an advocate for the unhoused during a freak Seattle blizzard.

We watch as Hunter is plunged into life after life, finally recognizing the futility of only looking out for #1 and understanding the part he must play in addressing the global climate crisis...if he ever gets another chance.

Recommended Daily Humanity

A checklist of human rights must include basic housing, universal healthcare, equitable funding for public schools, and tuition-free college and vocational training.

In addition to the basics, though, we need much more to fully thrive. Subsidized childcare, universal pre-K, a universal basic income, subsidized high-speed internet, net neutrality, fare-free public transit (plus *more* public transit), and medically assisted death for the terminally ill who want it.

None of this will matter, though, if we neglect to address the rapidly worsening climate crisis.

Sound expensive? It is.

But not as expensive as refusing to implement these changes. The cost of climate disasters each year has grown to staggering figures. And the cost of social and political upheaval from not meeting the needs of suffering workers, families, and individuals may surpass even that.

It's best we understand that the vast sums required to enact meaningful change are an investment which will pay off not only in some indeterminate future but in fact almost immediately. And without these adjustments to our lifestyles and values, there may very well not be a future capable of sustaining freedom and democracy…or even civilization itself.

The Camper Killings

When a homeless man is found murdered a few blocks from Morgan Beylerian's house in south Seattle, everyone seems to consider the body just so much additional trash to be cleared from the neighborhood. But Morgan liked the guy. They used to chat when Morgan brought Nick groceries once a week.

And the brutal way the man was killed reminds Morgan of their shared Mormon heritage, back when the faithful agreed to have their throats slit if they ever revealed temple secrets.

Did Nick's former wife take action when her ex-husband refused to grant a temple divorce? Did his murder have something to do with the public accusations that brought an end to his promising career?

Morgan does his best to investigate when no one else seems to care, but it isn't easy as a man living paycheck to paycheck himself, only able to pursue his investigation via public transit.

As he continues his search for the killer, Morgan's friends withdraw and his husband threatens to leave. When another homeless man is killed and Morgan is accused of the crime, things look even bleaker.

But his troubles aren't over yet.

Will Morgan find the killer before the killer finds him?

What Readers Have Said

Townsend's stories are "a gay *Portnoy's Complaint* of Mormonism. Salacious, sweet, sad, insightful, insulting, religiously ethnic, quirky-faithful, and funny."

D. Michael Quinn, author of *The Mormon Hierarchy: Origins of Power*

"Told from a believably conversational first-person perspective, [*The Abominable Gayman*'s] novelistic focus on Anderson's journey to thoughtful self-acceptance allows for greater character development than often seen in short stories, which makes this well-paced work rich and satisfying, and one of Townsend's strongest. An extremely important contribution to the field of Mormon fiction." Named to Kirkus Reviews' Best of 2011.

Kirkus Reviews

"The thirteen stories in *Mormon Underwear* capture this struggle [between Mormonism and homosexuality] with humor, sadness, insight, and sometimes shocking details....*Mormon Underwear* provides compelling stories, literally from the inside-out."

Niki D'Andrea, *Phoenix New Times*

"Townsend's lively writing style and engaging characters [in *Zombies for Jesus*] make for stories which force us to wake up, smell the (prohibited) coffee, and review our attitudes with regard to reading dogma so doggedly. These are tales which revel in the individual tics and quirks which make us human, Mormon or not, gay or not..."

A.J. Kirby, *The Short Review*

"The Rift," from *The Abominable Gayman*, is a "fascinating tale of an untenable situation...a *tour de force*."

David Lenson, editor, *The Massachusetts Review*

"Pronouncing the Apostrophe," from *The Golem of Rabbi Loew*, is "quiet and revealing, an intriguing tale..."

Sima Rabinowitz, Literary Magazine Review, *NewPages.com*

The Circumcision of God is "a collection of short stories that consider the imperfect, silenced majority of Mormons, who may in fact be [the Church's] best hope....[The book leaves] readers regretting the church's willingness to marginalize those who best exemplify its ideals: those who love fiercely despite all obstacles, who brave challenges at great personal risk and who always choose the hard, higher road."

Kirkus Reviews

In *Mormon Fairy Tales*, Johnny Townsend displays "both a wicked sense of irony and a deep well of compassion."

Kel Munger, *Sacramento News and Review*

Zombies for Jesus is "eerie, erotic, and magical."

Publishers Weekly

"While [Townsend's] many touching vignettes draw deeply from Mormon mythology, history, spirituality and culture, [*Mormon Fairy Tales*] is neither a gaudy act of proselytism nor angry protest literature from an ex-believer. Like all good fiction, his stories are simply about the joys, the hopes and the sorrows of people."

Kirkus Reviews

"In *Let the Faggots Burn* author Johnny Townsend restores this tragic event [the UpStairs Lounge fire] to its proper place in LGBT history and reminds us that the victims of the blaze were not just 'statistics,' but real people with real lives, families, and friends."

Jesse Monteagudo, *The Bilerico Project*

In *Let the Faggots Burn*, "Townsend's heart-rending descriptions of the victims...seem to [make them] come alive once more."

Kit Van Cleave, *OutSmart Magazine*

Marginal Mormons is "an irreverent, honest look at life outside the mainstream Mormon Church....Throughout his musings on sin and forgiveness, Townsend beautifully demonstrates his characters' internal, perhaps irreconcilable struggles....Rather than anger and disdain, he offers an honest portrayal of people searching for meaning and community in their lives, regardless of their life choices or secrets." Named to Kirkus Reviews' Best of 2012.

Kirkus Reviews

The stories in *The Mormon Victorian Society* "register the new openness and confidence of gay life in the age of same-sex marriage....What hasn't changed is Townsend's wry, conversational prose, his subtle evocations of character and social dynamics, and his deadpan humor. His warm empathy still glows in this intimate yet clear-eyed engagement with Mormon theology and folkways. Funny, shrewd and finely wrought dissections of the awkward contradictions—and surprising harmonies—between conscience and desire." Named to Kirkus Reviews' Best of 2013.

Kirkus Reviews

"This collection of short stories [*The Mormon Victorian Society*] featuring gay Mormon characters slammed [me] in the face from the first page, wrestled my heart and mind to the floor, and left me panting and wanting more by the end. Johnny Townsend has created so many memorable characters in such few pages. I went weeks thinking about this book. It truly touched me."

Tom Webb, *A Bear on Books*

Dragons of the Book of Mormon is an "entertaining collection….Townsend's prose is sharp, clear, and easy to read, and his characters are well rendered…"

Publishers Weekly

"The pre-eminent documenter of alternative Mormon lifestyles…Townsend has a deep understanding of his characters, and his limpid prose, dry humor and well-grounded (occasionally magical) realism make their spiritual conundrums both compelling and entertaining. [*Dragons of the Book of Mormon* is] [a]nother of Townsend's critical but affectionate and absorbing tours of Mormon discontent." Named to Kirkus Reviews' Best of 2014.

Kirkus Reviews

In *Gayrabian Nights*, "Townsend's prose is always limpid and evocative, and…he finds real drama and emotional depth in the most ordinary of lives."

Kirkus Reviews

Gayrabian Nights is a "complex revelation of how seriously soul damaging the denial of the true self can be."

Ryan Rhodes, author of *Free Electricity*

Gayrabian Nights "was easily the most original book I've read all year. Funny, touching, topical, and thoroughly enjoyable."

Rainbow Awards

Lying for the Lord is "one of the most gripping books that I've picked up for quite a while. I love the author's writing style, alternately cynical, humorous, biting, scathing, poignant, and touching…. This is the third book of his that I've read, and all are equally engaging. These are stories that need to be told, and the author does it in just the right way."

Heidi Alsop, *Ex-Mormon Foundation Board Member*

In *Lying for the Lord*, Townsend "gets under the skin of his characters to reveal their complexity and conflicts....shrewd, evocative [and] wryly humorous."

Kirkus Reviews

In *Missionaries Make the Best Companions*, "the author treats the clash between religious dogma and liberal humanism with vivid realism, sly humor, and subtle feeling as his characters try to figure out their true missions in life. Another of Townsend's rich dissections of Mormon failures and uncertainties..." Named to Kirkus Reviews' Best of 2015.

Kirkus Reviews

In *Invasion of the Spirit Snatchers*, "Townsend, a confident and practiced storyteller, skewers the hypocrisies and eccentricities of his characters with precision and affection. The outlandish framing narrative is the most consistent source of shock and humor, but the stories do much to ground the reader in the world—or former world—of the characters....A funny, charming tale about a group of Mormons facing the end of the world."

Kirkus Reviews

"Townsend's collection [*The Washing of Brains*] once again displays his limpid, naturalistic prose, skillful narrative chops, and his subtle insights into psychology...Well-crafted dispatches on the clash between religion and self-fulfillment..."

Kirkus Reviews

"While the author is generally at his best when working as a satirist, there are some fine, understated touches in these tales [*The Last Days Linger*] that will likely affect readers in subtle ways....readers should come away impressed by the deep empathy he shows for all his characters—even the homophobic ones."

Kirkus Reviews

"Written in a conversational style that often uses stories and personal anecdotes to reveal larger truths, this immensely approachable book [*Racism by Proxy*] skillfully serves its intended audience of White readers grappling with complex questions regarding race, history, and identity. The author's frequent references to the Church of Jesus Christ of Latter-day Saints may be too niche for readers unfamiliar with its idiosyncrasies, but Townsend generally strikes a perfect balance of humor, introspection, and reasoned arguments that will engage even skeptical readers."

Kirkus Reviews

Orgy at the STD Clinic portrays "an all-too real scenario that Townsend skewers to wincingly accurate proportions...[with] instant classic moments courtesy of his punchy, sassy, sexy lead character..."

Jim Piechota, *Bay Area Reporter*

Orgy at the STD Clinic is "…a triumph of humane sensibility. A richly textured saga that brilliantly captures the fraying social fabric of contemporary life." Named to Kirkus Reviews' Best Indie Books of 2022.

Kirkus Reviews

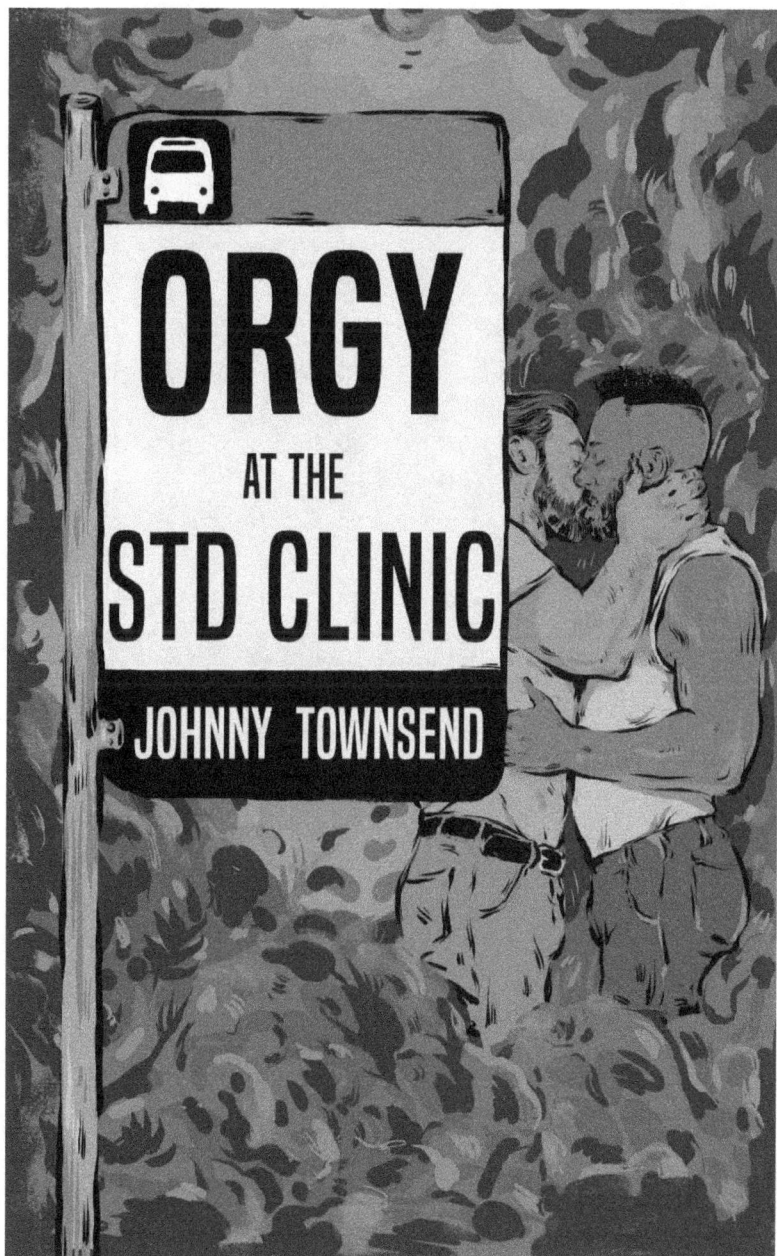

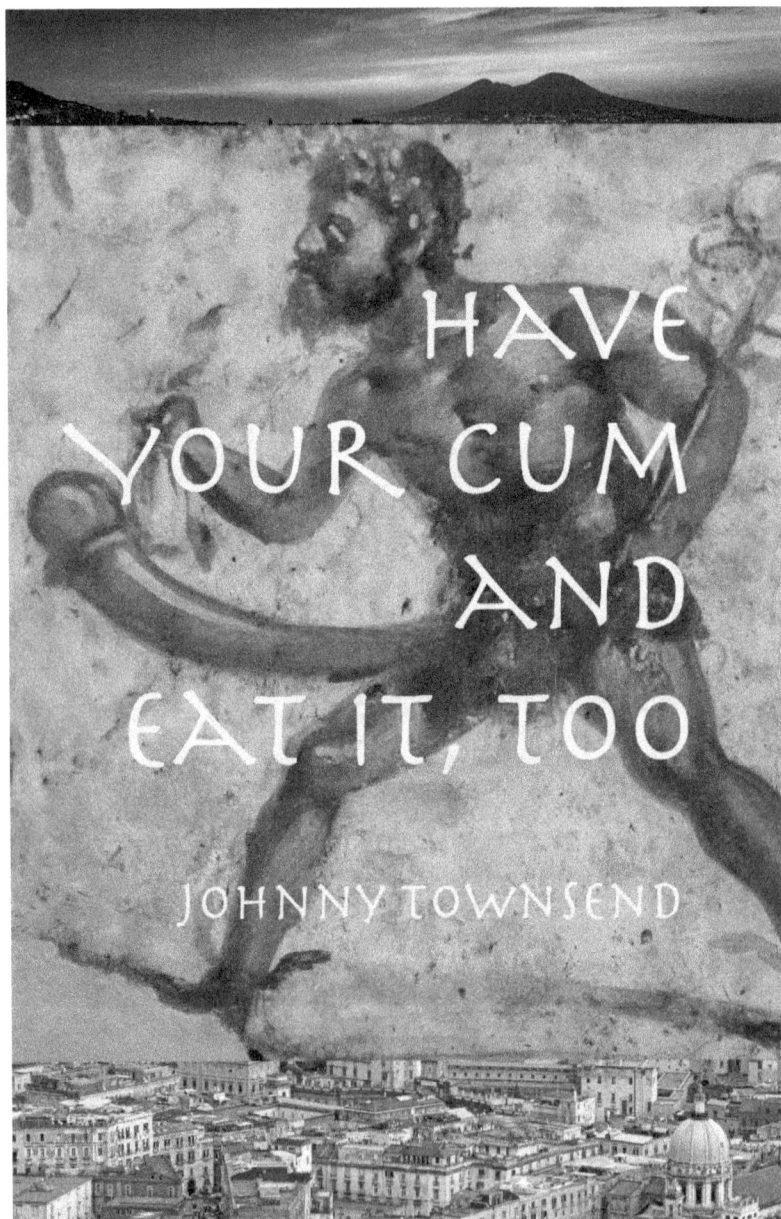

HAVE YOUR CUM AND EAT IT, TOO

JOHNNY TOWNSEND